Point-of-Purchase

DESIGN ANNUAL

8

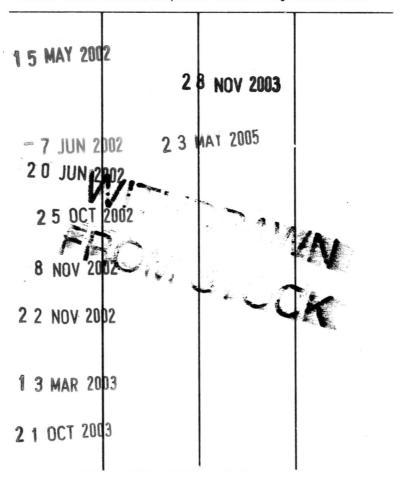

Point-of-Purchase

DESIGN ANNUAL

8

THE 43rd MERCHANDISING AWARDS

VISUAL REFERENCE PUBLICATIONS, INC. / NEW YORK

Visual Reference Publications, Inc.
302 Fifth Avenue
New York, NY 10001

Distributors to the trade in the United States and Canada
Watson-Guptill
770 Broadway
New York, NY 10003

Distributors outside the United States and Canada
HarperCollins International
10 East 53rd Street
New York, NY 10022-5299

Library of Congress Cataloging in Publication Data:
Main entry under title: Point-of-Purchase Design Annual No. 8

Printed in Hong Kong
ISBN 1-58471-051-9

Book design and type formatting by Bernard Schleifer

Contents

The POPAI Mission

POPAI is the international trade association of the point-of-purchase advertising industry. More than half of its corporate affiliate members are based outside the United States. POPAI is pursuing attainment of five strategic goals:

1) establish P-O-P advertising as a measured medium, on par with broadcast, print and other measured ad media;

2) capitalize on the increased use of technology for unprecedented opportunities for an expanded role for P-O-P advertising;

3) address members' changing needs as business becomes more global;

4) be more inclusive of those engaged in activities relevant to P-O-P advertising;

5) enjoy a business environment characterized by ethical business practices, expanded opportunities and preservation of rights as an advertising medium.

Introduction

WHAT ARE THE POPAI OMA AWARDS?

POPAI's Outstanding Merchandising Achievement (OMA) Awards recognize excellence in P-O-P advertising. Entries are judged by a blue-ribbon panel of clients, based on the display's ability to increase sales, obtain retail placements and work strategically to position the brand at the point of sale. For over forty years, POPAI's OMA Awards have recognized some of the most effective and original displays the industry has to offer, and is the premier awards recognition contests in the P-O-P advertising industry.

Entries are judged in two phases. In phase I, teams of judges review photographs and case histories of the entries in each category and assign preliminary scores. In phase II, the same judges view the actual entries on the POP Marketplace show floor and review scores for a final determination of winners.

In honor of their achievement, POPAI's OMA Awards winners receive statuettes which are gold, silver and bronze replicas of wooden cigar store Indians that once decorated the entrance of tobacco stores in the early Nineteenth Century. Carved by sailors from salvaged pieces of spars or masts from ships, these wooden figures are America's first known use of three-dimensional P-O-P advertising. Today, POPAI's OMA Awards statuette serves as a symbol of P-O-P's evolution from this modest beginning as a reminder of the intimate connection that P-O-P advertising has always had with consumer products.

POPAI's OMA Awards Contest is comprised of four contests that recognize excellence in P-O-P in different areas:

1. **OMA Contest:** recognizes the excellence of displays produced and placed anywhere in the world.

2. **Multinational Contest:** recognizes the merchandising excellence of displays produced and placed only outside of the United States, Europe and Japan.

3. **Technical Contest:** recognizes engineering excellence, innovative qualities or a unique solution to a design challenge.

4. **Display of the Year Contest:** recognizes the best in P-O-P advertising. A prestigious Display of the Year (DOY) Award is bestowed upon one gold winner in each of the following: Permanent OMA, Semi-Permanent OMA, Temporary OMA, and Multinational Contest.

Coming in March, 2001: POPAI has added five new retail categories and three new subcategories to the Signage Category.

Merchandising Awards Judges

OMA Contest Judges

Ms. Shelia Anderson
Mattel Toys Inc.

Ms. Maggie Ator
United Distillers & Vintners (UDVNA)

Mr. Steve Bartolucci
The Gillette Company

Ms. Susan Bell
Keebler Company

Mr. Matt Borgard
Barton Beers Ltd.

Mr. Bob Brisky
ICI Paints

Mr. Ted Brueggemann
Miller Brewing Company

Ms. Nancy Bruner
Kraft Foods

Ms. Lorraine Caldwell
The Raine Group

Mr. James Cantela
Elizabeth Arden

Mr. Greg Casey
Nintendo of America Inc.

Ms. Penny Cleare
Project Management Alliance

Mr. David Cook
RJ Reynolds Tobacco Company

Mr. Paul Cutlip
Florsheim Group Inc.

Ms. Barbara Daugherty
Frito-Lay, Inc.

Ms. Jennifer Dinehart
Corn Products International

Ms. Debbie Doerr
Wm. Wrigley Company

Mr. Thomas Donovan
Coty, Inc.

Ms. Bea Dorsey
Cooper Lighting

Mr. Robert Dyer
Eckerd Drug Corporation

Mr. Ronald Elowitz
Schering-Plough Health Care Products

Ms. Linda Feldman
Gibson Homans

Ms. Sandra M. Gallo
Miller Brewing Company

Mr. Robert Gentile
Warner-Lambert Adams Canada

Ms. Arlene Gerwin
United Distillers & Vintners (UDVNA)

Mr. Scott Greenberg
Skechers USA

Ms. Cynthia Harris
Sears Roebuck and Co.

Ms. Helen Hassler
Kraft Canada, Inc.

Mr. Jay Hawkinson
The Dial Corporation

Mr. Richard Kirwin
Snap-On Tools

Mr. Dennis Knaus
Diversified Merchandising Inc.

Mr. Kevin Kramnic
Barton Beers Ltd.

Mr. Stewart Lazares
The Gillette Company

Ms. Andrea L. Martin
E & J Gallo Winery

Ms. Rosemary McDaniel
Bayer Corporation

Ms. Anne Norris
Timex Corporation

Mr. Bernardino Reynoso
E & J Gallo Winery

Ms. JoLynn Rogers
Square D

Mr. George Rutkowski
B & K Industries

Ms. Marilyn Rutkowski
Buddy Products

Ms. Sharon Ruzga
Ideal Industries

Mr. Dan Vnencak
Nabisco Biscuit Company

Mr. Michael Wang
Beckett Corporation

Ms. Deana Whitman
Frito-Lay, Inc.

Mr. Kurt Witzel
Anheuser-Busch Inc.

Mr. Randy Young
GE Lighting

Multinational Contest Judges

Mr. Stephen De Lorenzo
Coca-Cola South Pacific Pty Limited

Mr. Jorge Dionne Espinsa
Reebok De Mexico

Mr. Patrick Good
Energizer Canada

Mr. Hector Luis Mendoza Lavin
Unilever-Pond's Mexico

Mr. Manuel Tonatiuh Navarro Mastache
Allied Domecq Spirits and Wine, Mexico

Mr. Arturo Amezcua Sandoval
Grupo Gamesa, S.A. De C.V.

Ms. Debbie Schubert
Snacks and Brands Australia

Ms. Amanda Senior
Australia

Mr. Chris Steele
Cheltenham and Glouchester Plc.

Ms. Linda Woods
Maple Leaf Consumer Foods

Ms. Karen Woolley
Quaker Oats Company of Canada Ltd.

Technical Contest Judges

Mr. Bill Abene
Panel Prints Inc.

Mr. William Baucom
E-B Display Co. Inc.

Mr. Herm Buechel
Ivex Packaging

Ms. Diana Campbell
Smurfit-Stone Display Group

Mr. Richard M. Carrigan Jr.
United Displaycraft

Mr. Joseph Fish
Hankscraft Motors, Inc.

Mr. Mike Friedman
Trans World Marketing

Mr. Mark Stanton
Trans World Marketing

Mr. Jack Wuensch
Rand Display Inc.

Display of the Year Judges

Ms. Shelia Anderson
Mattel Toys

Mr. Steve Bartolucci
The Gillette Company

Mr. Ted Brueggemann
Miller Brewing Company

Ms. Nancy Bruner
Kraft Foods

Mr. Greg Casey
Nintendo of America Inc.

Ms. Penny Cleare
Project Management Alliance

Ms. Arlene Gerwin
United Distillers & Vintners

Ms. Sandra Gallo
Miller Brewing Company

Mr. Jay Hawkinson
The Dial Corporation

Mr. Richard Kirwin
Snap-On Tools

Mr. Michael Lanaghan
Wm. Wrigley Jr. Company

Mr. Stewart Lazares
The Gillette Company

Ms. Andrea Martin
E&J Gallo Winery

Display of the Year
Contest Winners

TEMPORARY DISPLAY OF THE YEAR WINNER

TITLE
Jim Beam Holiday Guitar

CLIENT
Jim Beam Brands Co.

ENTRANT
Rapid Displays
Chicago, IL

SUB-CATEGORY
Distilled Spirits - Illuminated or Motion

DIVISION
Temporary

OBJECTIVES
Attract customer interest and increase sales of Jim Beam during the holiday season using the theme Turn Up Your Holidays.

MATERIALS
100# 4-color process litho mounted to .045 black chipboard, 100# 4-color process litho mounted to 3/16 black foam core, .024 4-color process die cut.

TEMPORARY DISPLAY OF THE YEAR WINNER

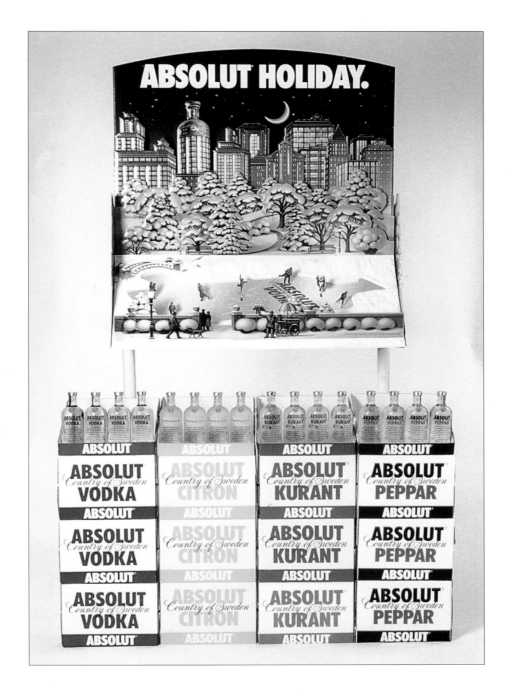

TITLE
Absolut 1999 Holiday Mega Mass Display

CLIENT
Seagram Americas

ENRANT
Upshot
Chicago, IL

SUB-CATEGORY
Distilled Spirits - Illuminated or Motion

DIVISION
Temporary

OBJECTIVES
Secure retail floor space during the peak holiday sales period, spark impulse sales and maintain Absolut's high standard of quality.

MATERIALS
Litho Printing, Corrogate, Foam-core, Silver Mylar, Vacuform plastic, Twinkling lights, D batteries

SALES PROMOTION DISPLAY OF THE YEAR WINNER

Press Kit

Counter Card

Standee

TITLE
Donkey Kong 64 Sales Promotion

CLIENT
Nintendo of America

ENTRANT
The Corporate Image
Seattle, WA

SUB-CATEGORY
National

DIVISION
Semi-Permanent

OBJECTIVES
This promotion is designed to create excitement for the new three dimensional Donkey Kong 64 by using multi-dimensional displays and press kit.

MATERIALS
4/color process. 80# gloss book laminated to B Flute 100# gloss book laminated to foamcore. Molded plastic easel.

MULTINATIONAL DISPLAY OF THE YEAR WINNER

TITLE
Kit Kat Bonus Break Merchandiser

CLIENT
Nestle Confectionery Ltd

ENTRANT
Ace Print & Display Pty Ltd
Revesby, Australia

SUB-CATEGORY
Multinational

DIVISION
Temporary

OBJECTIVES
Increase sales of Kit Kat in Bonus Break consumer activity. Extend the chocolate season into summer by communicating the appeal of KIT KAT in fridges.

MATERIALS
All corrugated cardboard. Shroud litho printed and laminated to B Flute. Riser screen printed on B/C Twin Cushion. Shelves screen printed on B Flute.

PERMANENT DISPLAY OF THE YEAR WINNER

TITLE
Everland Kid City Interactive Kiosk

CLIENT
Word Entertainment

ENRANT
Trans World Marketing
East Rutherford, NJ

SUB-CATEGORY
Interactive

DIVISION
Permanent

OBJECTIVES
Provide a state-of-the-art destination display and retail selling center for the Everland Music product line.

MATERIALS
Illumination, motion, vacuum forming, injection molding, plexi, slatwall, wire, Macintosh G3 computer and Phillips touch screen monitor.

POPAI's Outstanding Merchandising Achievement (OMA) Awards Contest

The OMA Contest recognizes merchandising excellence of displays produced and placed anywhere in the world.

AWARD
Gold

TITLE
Coors Light Racing Tire Neon

CLIENT
The Integer Group for Coors Brewing

ENTRANT
Everbrite, Inc.
Greenfield, WI

SUB-CATEGORY
Off-Premise - Illuminated or Motion

DIVISION
Permanent

AWARD
Gold

TITLE
MGD Keg On Ice Pool Table Lamp

CLIENT
Miller Brewing Company

ENTRANT
Everbrite, Inc.
Greenfield, WI

SUB-CATEGORY
On-Premise - Illuminated or Motion

DIVISION
Permanent

AWARD
Gold

TITLE
Bud 1 Airship Pool Table Light

CLIENT
Anheuser-Busch Inc.

ENTRANT
Grimm Industries, Inc.
Fairview, PA

SUB-CATEGORY
On-Premise - Illuminated or Motion

DIVISION
Permanent

AWARD
Gold

TITLE
Sam Adams Giant Six Pack Carrier

CLIENT
Boston Beer Company

ENTRANT
C.D. Baird & Co., Inc.
West Allis, WI

SUB-CATEGORY
Off-Premise - Non-Illuminated
or Non-Motion

DIVISION
Temporary

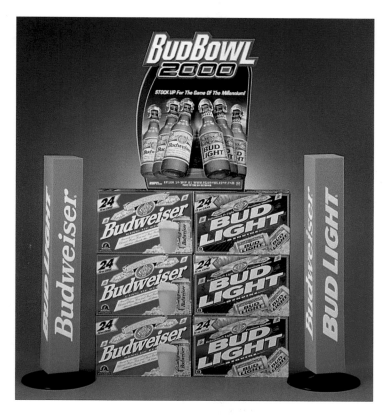

AWARD
Gold

TITLE
Bud Bowl Motion Display
2000/End Zone Wobbler

CLIENT
Anheuser-Busch, Inc.

ENTRANT
Rapid Displays
Chicago, IL

SUB-CATEGORY
On-Premise - Illuminated or Motion

DIVISION
Temporary

AWARD
Silver

TITLE
MGD Kegs to Go

CLIENT
Miller Brewing Company

ENTRANT
Trans World Marketing
East Rutherford, NJ

SUB-CATEGORY
Off-Premise - Non-Illuminated
or Non-Motion

DIVISION
Permanent

AWARD
Silver

TITLE
Budweiser Millennium Program

CLIENT
Anheuser-Busch, Inc.

ENTRANT
Everbrite, Inc.
Greenfield, WI

SUB-CATEGORY
On-Premise - Illuminated or
Motion

DIVISION
Permanent

AWARD
Silver

TITLE
Tequiza Illuminated
Lenticular 3-D Sign

CLIENT
Anheuser-Busch, Inc.

ENTRANT
Phoenix Display/
International Paper
Thorofare, NJ

SUB-CATEGORY
On-Premise - Illuminated
or Motion

DIVISION
Permanent

AWARD
Silver

TITLE
Budweiser/ESPN Sports Casestacker

CLIENT
Anheuser-Busch, Inc.

ENTRANT
Phoenix Display/International Paper
Thorofare, NJ

SUB-CATEGORY
Off-Premise - Non-Illuminated or Non-Motion

DIVISION
Semi-Permanent

AWARD
Silver

TITLE
Miller Brewing Route Truck Display

CLIENT
Miller Brewing Company

ENTRANT
Paul Flum Ideas, Inc.
Saint Louis, MO

SUB-CATEGORY
On-Premise - Non-Illuminated or
Non-Motion

DIVISION
Semi-Permanent

AWARD
Silver

TITLE
Bud 4th of July Motion

CLIENT
Anheuser-Busch Inc.

ENTRANT
Rapid Displays
Chicago, IL

SUB-CATEGORY
Off-Premise - Illuminated or Motion

DIVISION
Temporary

AWARD
Silver

TITLE
Bud/Mich Family Oktoberfest Aisle Spinner

CLIENT
Anheuser-Busch Inc.

ENTRANT
Chesapeake Display & Packaging
Winston Salem, NC

SUB-CATEGORY
Off-Premise - Non-Illuminated or Non-
Motion

DIVISION
Temporary

AWARD
Silver

TITLE
Bud Family St. Pats Sticker Table Tent

CLIENT
Anheuser-Busch, Inc.

ENTRANT
Anheuser-Busch, Inc.
Saint Louis, MO

SUB-CATEGORY
On-Premise - Non-Illuminated
or Non-Motion

DIVISION
Temporary

AWARD
Bronze

TITLE
Miller High Life Edgelit Sign

CLIENT
Miller Brewing Company

ENTRANT
Everbrite, Inc.
Greenfield, WI

SUB-CATEGORY
Off-Premise - Illuminated or Motion

DIVISION
Permanent

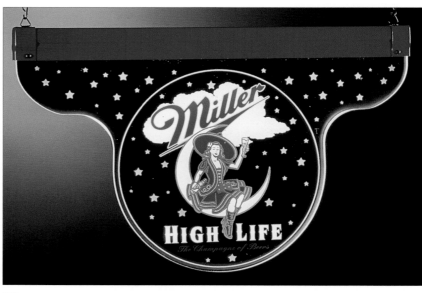

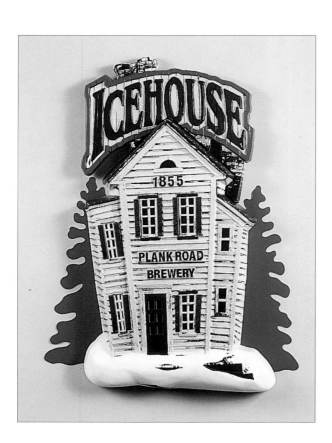

AWARD
Bronze

TITLE
Icehouse Non-Illuminated Wall Sign

CLIENT
Plank Road Brewery

ENTRANT
KCS Industries, Inc.
Hartland, WI

SUB-CATEGORY
Off-Premise - Non-Illuminated or Non-Motion

DIVISION
Permanent

AWARD
Bronze

TITLE
Budweiser Tiffany Hanging Lamp

CLIENT
Anheuser-Busch Inc.

ENTRANT
Gage In-Store Marketing
Minneapolis, MN

SUB-CATEGORY
On-Premise - Illuminated or Motion

DIVISION
Permanent

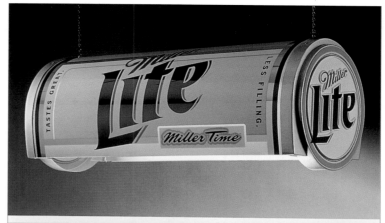

AWARD
Bronze

TITLE
Miller Lite Lamp Program

CLIENT
Miller Brewing Company

ENTRANT
Everbrite, Inc.
Greenfield, WI

SUB-CATEGORY
On-Premise - Illuminated or Motion

DIVISION
Permanent

AWARD
Bronze

TITLE
Miller High Life Rotating Refrig. Back Bar

CLIENT
Miller Brewing Company

ENTRANT
KCS Industries, Inc.
Hartland, WI

SUB-CATEGORY
On-Premise - Illuminated or Motion

DIVISION
Permanent

AWARD
Bronze

TITLE
Illuminated Asahi Bottle Display with Halo

CLIENT
Asahi Beer Europe Ltd

ENTRANT
Westiform International GmbH
Ortenberg, Germany

SUB-CATEGORY
On-Premise - Illuminated or Motion

DIVISION
Permanent

AWARD
Bronze

TITLE
MGD Multi-Tool

CLIENT
Miller Brewing Company

ENTRANT
Trans World Marketing
East Rutherford, NJ

SUB-CATEGORY
On-Premise - Non-Illuminated
or Non-Motion

DIVISION
Permanent

AWARD
Bronze

TITLE
Coors Light July Fourth Dominator

CLIENT
The Integer Group

ENTRANT
C.D. Baird & Co., Inc.
West Allis, WI

SUB-CATEGORY
Off-Premise - Illuminated or Motion

DIVISION
Temporary

AWARD
Bronze

TITLE
Coors ShowCase TM

CLIENT
Coors Brewing Company

ENTRANT
Inland Consumer
Packaging and Displays
Indianapolis, IN

SUB-CATEGORY
Off-Premise - Illuminated
or Motion

DIVISION
Temporary

AWARD
Bronze

TITLE
Red Dog Snack Display

CLIENT
Plank Road Brewery

ENTRANT
Great Northern Corporation
Racine, WI

SUB-CATEGORY
Off-Premise - Non-Illuminated
or Non-Motion

DIVISION
Temporary

AWARD
Bronze

TITLE
Anheuser-Busch Lighted Christmas Tree

CLIENT
Anheuser-Busch, Inc.

ENTRANT
Phoenix Display/International Paper
Thorofare, NJ

SUB-CATEGORY
Off-Premise - Non-Illuminated or Non-Motion

DIVISION
Temporary

AWARD
Gold

TITLE
Gordon's Schweppes Display

CLIENT
Moet Hennessy UDV France

ENTRANT
Prisme
Suresnes, France

SUB-CATEGORY
Distilled Spirits - Illuminated
or Motion

DIVISION
Permanent

AWARD
Gold

TITLE
Bacardi Five Brands Display

CLIENT
Bacardi-Martini Promotions

ENTRANT
Smurfit-Stone Display Group
Richmond, VA

SUB-CATEGORY
Distilled Spirits -
Non-Illuminated or Non-Motion

DIVISION
Semi-Permanent

AWARD
Gold

TITLE
Bombay Multi-case Acrylic Rack

CLIENT
Bacardi Martini

ENTRANT
Bish Creative Display
Lake Zurich, IL

SUB-CATEGORY
Distilled Spirits - Non-
Illuminated or Non-Motion

DIVISION
Permanent

AWARD
Gold/Display-of-the-Year

TITLE
Jim Beam Holiday Guitar

CLIENT
Jim Beam Brands Co.

ENTRANT
Rapid Displays
Chicago, IL

SUB-CATEGORY
Distilled Spirits - Illuminated or Motion

DIVISION
Temporary

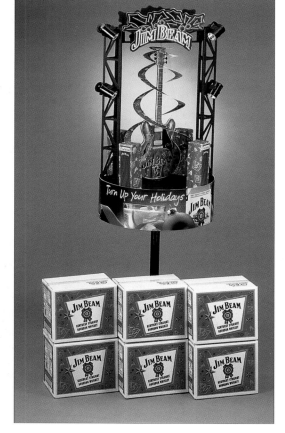

AWARD
Gold/Display-of-the-Year

TITLE
Absolut 1999 Holiday Mega
Mass Display

CLIENT
Seagram Americas

ENTRANT
Upshot
Chicago, IL

SUB-CATEGORY
Distilled Spirits - Illuminated or
Motion

DIVISION
Temporary

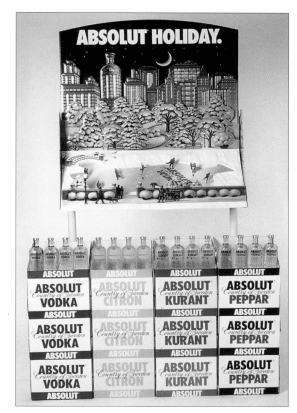

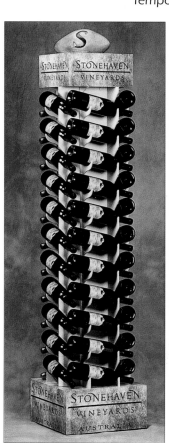

AWARD
Silver

TITLE
Stone Haven Floor
Display (4 Case)

CLIENT
Banfi Vintners

ENTRANT
Flair Display Inc.
Bronx, NY

SUB-CATEGORY
Cordials and Wines

DIVISION
Permanent

AWARD
Silver

TITLE
Baileys Display Stand

CLIENT
United Distillers and Vintners

ENTRANT
Marketing Drive pty ltd.
Sydney, Australia

SUB-CATEGORY
Distilled Spirits -
Illuminated or Motion

DIVISION
Permanent

AWARD
Silver

TITLE
Grey Goose Floor Display

CLIENT
Sidney Frank Importing Co., Inc.

ENTRANT
Flair Display Inc.
Bronx, NY

SUB-CATEGORY
Distilled Spirits - Non-Illuminated
or Non-Motion

DIVISION
Permanent

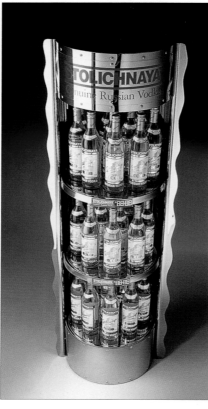

AWARD
Silver

TITLE
Solichnaya Display Stand

CLIENT
United Distillers and Vintners

ENTRANT
Marketing Drive pty ltd.
Sydney, Australia

SUB-CATEGORY
Distilled Spirits - Non-
Illuminated or Non-Motion

DIVISION
Permanent

AWARD
Silver

TITLE
Ruffino Cart

CLIENT
Schieffelin & Somerset Co., Inc.

ENTRANT
Flair Display Inc.
Bronx, NY

SUB-CATEGORY
Cordials and Wines

DIVISION
Semi-Permanent

AWARD
Silver

TITLE
Ecco Domani Boat Mass

CLIENT
E & J Gallo Winery

ENTRANT
Bert-Co Graphics
Los Angeles, CA

SUB-CATEGORY
Cordials and Wines

DIVISION
Temporary

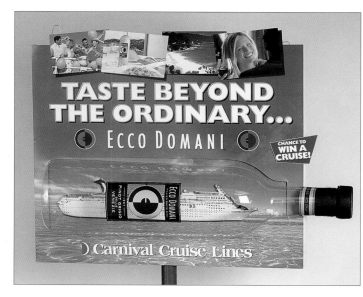

AWARD
Silver

TITLE
Tanqueray Holiday '99 Floor Display

CLIENT
Schieffelin & Somerset Co., Inc.

ENTRANT
Display Products N.A. Inc.
Yaphank, NY

SUB-CATEGORY
Distilled Spirits - Non-Illuminated
or Non-Motion

DIVISION
Temporary

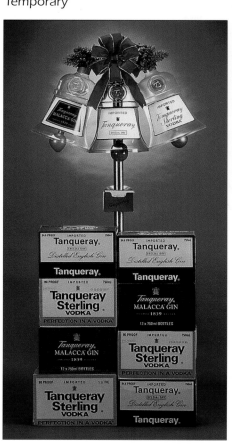

AWARD
Silver

TITLE
Bacardi Christmas Motion Display

CLIENT
Bacardi Martini

ENTRANT
Bish Creative Display
Lake Zurich, IL

SUB-CATEGORY
Distilled Spirits - Illuminated or Motion

DIVISION
Temporary

AWARD
Bronze

TITLE
Danzante Wine Rack

CLIENT
Robert Mondavi Winery

ENTRANT
Baer Enterprises
Livermore, CA

SUB-CATEGORY
Cordials and Wines

DIVISION
Permanent

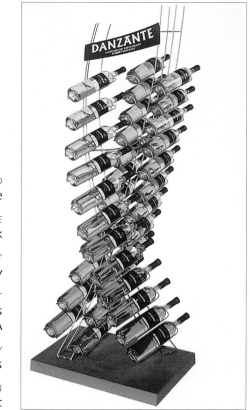

AWARD
Bronze

TITLE
Gossamer Bay 3 Bottle Counter Display

CLIENT
E. & J. Gallo Winery

ENTRANT
MBH Presentations, Inc. Floral Park, NY

SUB-CATEGORY
Cordials and Wines

DIVISION
Permanent

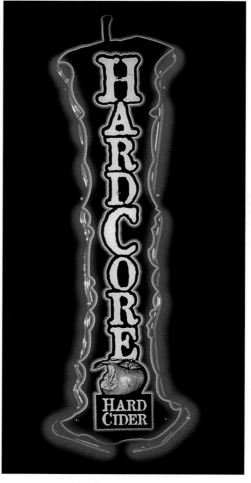

AWARD
Bronze

TITLE
Hard Core Cider Neon

CLIENT
The Boston Beer Company

ENTRANT
Everbrite, Inc. Greenfield, WI

SUB-CATEGORY
Distilled Spirits - Illuminated or Motion

DIVISION
Permanent

AWARD
Bronze

TITLE
Moet Millennium Window Display

CLIENT
Schieffelin & Somerset & Co., Inc.

ENTRANT
Flair Display Inc. Bronx, NY

SUB-CATEGORY
Distilled Spirits - Illuminated or Motion

DIVISION
Permanent

AWARD
Bronze

TITLE
Soho Display

CLIENT
Pernod S.A.

ENTRANT
Prisme
Suresnes, France

SUB-CATEGORY
Distilled Spirits -
Illuminated or Motion

DIVISION
Permanent

AWARD
Bronze

TITLE
Classic Malts Glorifier

CLIENT
Schieffelin & Somerset & Co., Inc.

ENTRANT
Flair Display Inc.
Bronx, NY

SUB-CATEGORY
Distilled Spirits - Non-Illuminated
or Non-Motion

DIVISION
Permanent

AWARD
Bronze

TITLE
Finlandia Martini Glasses

CLIENT
Brown - Forman Corporation

ENTRANT
Heritage Sign & Display
Nesquehoning, PA

SUB-CATEGORY
Distilled Spirits - Non-Illuminated
or Non-Motion

DIVISION
Permanent

AWARD
Bronze

TITLE
Strongbow White Barbed Wire
Bottle Holder

CLIENT
Bulmer Australia Limited

ENTRANT
Reid Lalor Displays
Kirrawee, N.S.W., Australia

SUB-CATEGORY
Distilled Spirits - Non-Illuminated
or Non-Motion

DIVISION
Permanent

AWARD
Bronze

TITLE
Brown-Forman Spirit's
Of The World Rack

CLIENT
Brown-Forman Beverage Company

ENTRANT
MBH Presentations, Inc.
Floral Park, NY

SUB-CATEGORY
Distilled Spirits - Non-Illuminated
or Non-Motion

DIVISION
Semi-Permanent

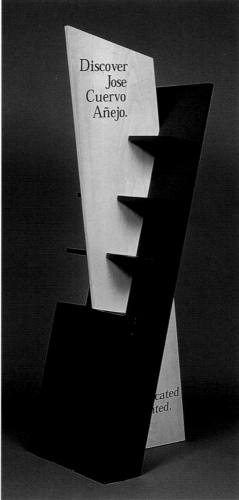

AWARD
Bronze

TITLE
Jose Cuervo Añejo Floorstand

CLIENT
United Distillers and Vinters

ENTRANT
Ultimate Display Industries
Jamaica, NY

SUB-CATEGORY
Distilled Spirits - Non-Illuminated
or Non-Motion

DIVISION
Permanent

AWARD
Bronze

TITLE
Glen Ellen Wines Holiday Mass
Merchandiser

CLIENT
United Distillers & Vintners North America

ENTRANT
C.D. Baird & Co., Inc.
West Allis, WI

SUB-CATEGORY
Cordials and Wines

DIVISION
Temporary

AWARD
Bronze

TITLE
Beaulieu Vineyards Summer Stacker

CLIENT
Glen Ellen Winery

ENTRANT
Phoenix Display/International Paper
Thorofare, NJ

SUB-CATEGORY
Cordials and Wines

DIVISION
Temporary

AWARD
Bronze

TITLE
Dewar's Holiday Mass Merchandiser

CLIENT
Bacardi Martini Promotions

ENTRANT
Protagon Display Inc.
Scarborough, ON, Canada

SUB-CATEGORY
Distilled Spirits - Illuminated or Motion

DIVISION
Temporary

AWARD
Bronze

TITLE
Jack Daniel's Holiday 3-D Case Card

CLIENT
Draft WorldWide for Brown Foreman

ENTRANT
Rapid Displays
Chicago, IL

SUB-CATEGORY
Distilled Spirits - Non-Illuminated
or Non-Motion

DIVISION
Temporary

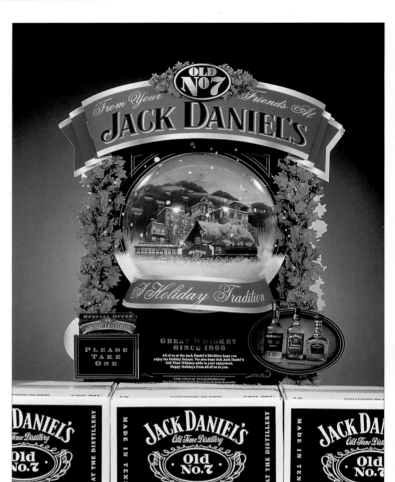

AWARD
Bronze

TITLE
Absolut Citron Pole Display

CLIENT
Seagram Americas

ENTRANT
Upshot
Chicago, IL

SUB-CATEGORY
Distilled Spirits - Non-
Illuminated or Non-Motion

DIVISION
Temporary

AWARD
Bronze

TITLE
Scotsfest 2000 Mega
Display

CLIENT
Schieffelin & Somerset Co., Inc.

ENTRANT
York Display and Manhattan
Marketing Ensemble
Brooklyn, NY

SUB-CATEGORY
Distilled Spirits - Non-Illuminated
or Non-Motion

DIVISION
Temporary

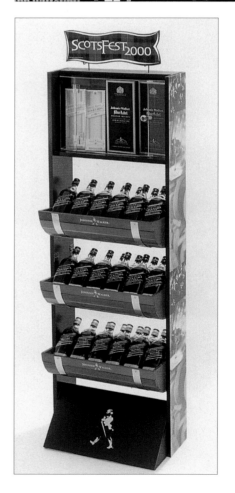

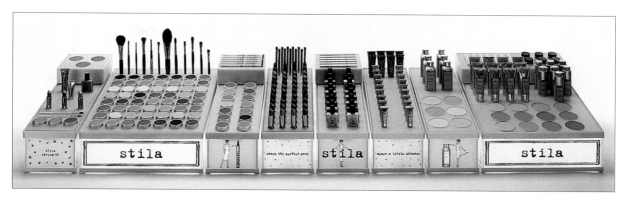

AWARD
Gold

TITLE
Beautiful By Natural Color
Playstation

CLIENT
Bath and Body Works

ENTRANT
The Royal Promotion Group
New York, NY

SUB-CATEGORY
Multiple Product Line
Merchandisers

DIVISION
Permanent

AWARD
Gold

TITLE
Stila Illuminated Full Line
Display System

CLIENT
Stila Cosmetics

ENTRANT
The Royal Promotion Group
New York, NY

SUB-CATEGORY
Multiple Product Line Merchandisers

DIVISION
Permanent

AWARD
Gold

TITLE
Colorstay Liquid Lip
Floorstand

CLIENT
Revlon Inc.

ENTRANT
Advertising Display
Company
Lyndhurst, NJ

SUB-CATEGORY
Single Product Line
Merchandisers

DIVISION
Temporary

AWARD
Gold

TITLE
Lancôme Saks Spring 2000

CLIENT
Lancôme

ENTRANT
Promotional Development Inc.
Brooklyn, NY

SUB-CATEGORY
Testers

DIVISION
Semi-Permanent

AWARD
Gold

TITLE
Max Factor Gift Set

CLIENT
Procter & Gamble Cosmetics

ENTRANT
Rock-Tenn Company/ Alliance Group
Winston Salem, NC

SUB-CATEGORY
Single Product Line Merchandisers

DIVISION
Temporary

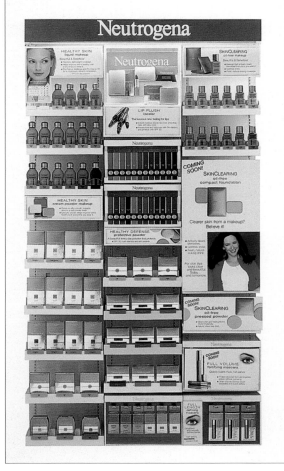

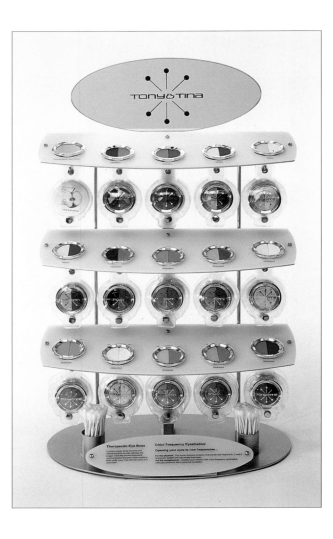

AWARD
Silver

TITLE
Tony and Tina Eyeshadow
Merchandiser

CLIENT
Tony and Tina Cosmetics

ENTRANT
The Royal Promotion Group
New York, NY

SUB-CATEGORY
Single Product Line Merchandisers

DIVISION
Permanent

AWARD
Silver

TITLE
Neutrogena Cosmetics
Merchandising System

CLIENT
Neutrogena Cosmetics

ENTRANT
Display Systems
Maspeth, NY

SUB-CATEGORY
Multiple Product Line Merchandisers

DIVISION
Permanent

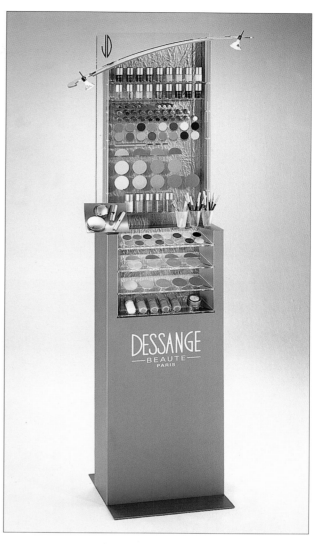

AWARD
Silver

TITLE
Dessange Makeup
General Tester Stand

CLIENT
Jacques Dessange

ENTRANT
Diam Groupe
Les Mureaux, Cedex, France

SUB-CATEGORY
Testers

DIVISION
Permanent

AWARD
Silver

TITLE
Estée Lauder Holiday Color Story

CLIENT
Estée Lauder, Inc.

ENTRANT
Consumer Promotions International
Mount Vernon, NY

SUB-CATEGORY
Multiple Product Line Merchandisers

DIVISION
Semi-Permanent

AWARD
Silver

TITLE
Maybelline Express Makeup 3 in 1

CLIENT
Maybelline, Inc.

ENTRANT
Ultimate Display Industries
Jamaica, NY

SUB-CATEGORY
Single Product Line
Merchandisers

DIVISION
Semi-Permanent

AWARD
Silver

TITLE
Origins Color Palette
Shimmer Unit

CLIENT
Estée Lauder

ENTRANT
P.O.P. Displays International
Woodside, NY

SUB-CATEGORY
Testers

DIVISION
Semi-Permanent

AWARD
Bronze

TITLE
Max Factor Italy Standa Counter
Merchandiser

CLIENT
Procter & Gamble

ENTRANT
Diam Group
Loughborough, Leicester, United Kingdom

SUB-CATEGORY
Multiple Product Line Merchandisers

DIVISION
Permanent

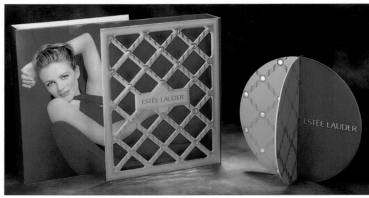

AWARD
Silver

TITLE
Estée Lauder
Christmas Lattice

CLIENT
Estée Lauder USA

ENTRANT
Clarke Productions
Dundas, ON, Canada

SUB-CATEGORY
Multiple Product Line
Merchandisers

DIVISION
Temporary

AWARD
Silver

TITLE
L'Oréal On the Loose
Counter Display

CLIENT
L'Oréal Canada

ENTRANT
Point 1 Displays Inc.
Montreal, Quebec, Canada

SUB-CATEGORY
Single Product Line Merchandisers

DIVISION
Temporary

AWARD
Bronze

TITLE
Estée Lauder Skincare Full Line Tester

CLIENT
Estée Lauder Inc.

ENTRANT
IDMD Design and Manufacturing Inc.
Toronto, ON, Canada

SUB-CATEGORY
Multiple Product Line Merchandisers

DIVISION
Permanent

AWARD
Bronze

TITLE
Max Factor Scandinavian
1.2m x 1.65m Gondola

CLIENT
Procter & Gamble

ENTRANT
Diam Group
Loughborough, Leicester,
United Kingdom

SUB-CATEGORY
Multiple Product Line
Merchandisers

DIVISION
Permanent

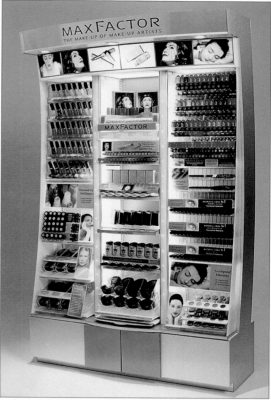

AWARD
Bronze

TITLE
Chanel Single Product
Counter Display

CLIENT
Chanel

ENTRANT
Consumer Promotions
International
Mount Vernon, NY

SUB-CATEGORY
Single Product Line
Merchandisers

DIVISION
Permanent

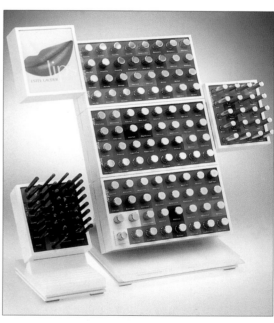

AWARD
Bronze

TITLE
Estée Lauder Total Lip Category

CLIENT
Estée Lauder, Inc.

ENTRANT
Consumer Promotions International
Mount Vernon, NY

SUB-CATEGORY
Single Product Line Merchandisers

DIVISION
Permanent

AWARD
Bronze

TITLE
Chanel Display Program

CLIENT
Chanel

ENTRANT
Consumer Promotions International
Mount Vernon, NY

SUB-CATEGORY
Testers

DIVISION
Permanent

AWARD
Bronze

TITLE
Prescriptives Foundation
Tester Tower

CLIENT
Prescriptives

ENTRANT
IDMD Manufacturing Inc.
Toronto, ON, Canada

SUB-CATEGORY
Testers

DIVISION
Permanent

AWARD
Bronze

TITLE
YSL Makeup
General Tester Stand

CLIENT
YSL

ENTRANT
Diam Groupe
Les Mureaux, Cedex, France

SUB-CATEGORY
Testers

DIVISION
Permanent

AWARD
Bronze

TITLE
Elizabeth Arden Fall '99 Color Story

CLIENT
Elizabeth Arden, Inc.

ENTRANT
Mechtronics Corporation
Stamford, CT

SUB-CATEGORY
Single Product Line Merchandisers

DIVISION
Semi-Permanent

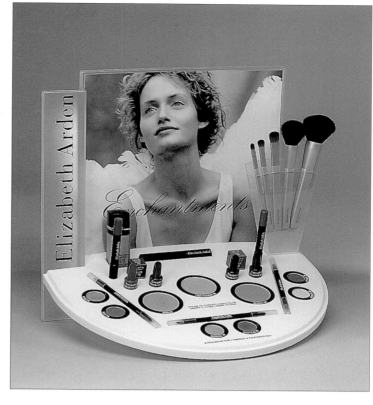

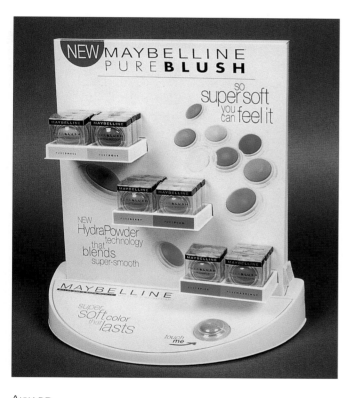

AWARD
Bronze

TITLE
Maybelline Pure Blush Launch

CLIENT
Maybelline, Inc.

ENTRANT
Ultimate Display Industries
Jamaica, NY

SUB-CATEGORY
Single Product Line
Merchandisers

DIVISION
Semi-Permanent

AWARD
Bronze

TITLE
Maybelline Hydra Time Launch

CLIENT
Maybelline, Inc.

ENTRANT
Ultimate Display Industries
Jamaica, NY

SUB-CATEGORY
Single Product Line
Merchandisers

DIVISION
Semi-Permanent

AWARD
Bronze

TITLE
Estée Lauder Hot Fuschia Look

CLIENT
Estée Lauder IMD

ENTRANT
Diam Groupe
Les Mureaux, Cedex, France

SUB-CATEGORY
Testers

DIVISION
Semi-Permanent

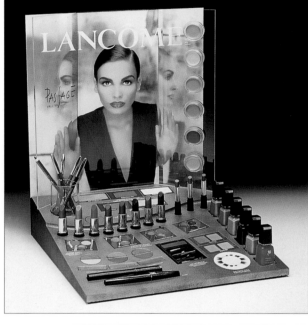

AWARD
Bronze

TITLE
Lancôme Spring 2000
"Pollen" Display

CLIENT
Lancôme, Inc.

ENTRANT
P.O.P. Displays International
Woodside, NY

SUB-CATEGORY
Testers

DIVISION
Semi-Permanent

AWARD
Bronze

TITLE
Lancôme-Fall '99 Passage Promo
Display

CLIENT
Lancôme, Inc.

ENTRANT
P.O.P. Displays International
Woodside, NY

TESTERS
Sub-Category

DIVISION
Semi-Permanent

AWARD
Bronze

TITLE
Almay One Coat Refrigerators

CLIENT
Revlon Inc.

ENTRANT
Advertising Display Company
Lyndhurst, NJ

SUB-CATEGORY
Multiple Product Line
Merchandisers

DIVISION
Temporary

AWARD
Bronze

TITLE
L'Oréal Summer Shade Dispaly

CLIENT
L'Oréal, Inc.

ENTRANT
Display Producers, Inc.
Bronx, NY

SUB-CATEGORY
Multiple Product Line Merchandisers

DIVISION
Temporary

AWARD
Bronze

TITLE
Olay Cosmetics Fall "Live in Cashmere" Program

CLIENT
Procter & Gamble

ENTRANT
Rock-Tenn Company/ Alliance Group
Winston Salem, NC

SUB-CATEGORY
Multiple Product Line Merchandisers

DIVISION
Temporary

AWARD
Bronze

TITLE
L'Oréal Hydra Soft Display

CLIENT
L'Oréal, Inc.

ENTRANT
Display Producers, Inc.
Bronx, NY

SUB-CATEGORY
Single Product Line Merchandisers

DIVISION
Temporary

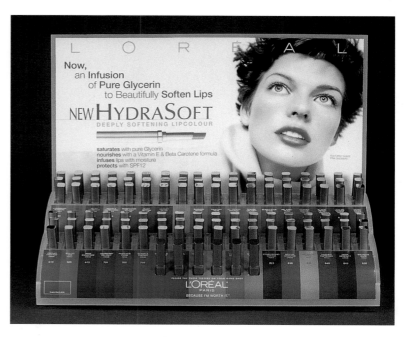

AWARD
Gold

TITLE
RCA Digital Entertainment Center

CLIENT
RadioShack

ENTRANT
Trans World Marketing
East Rutherford, NJ

SUB-CATEGORY
Home Entertainment - Interactive,
Motion or Illuminated (including radios,
TVs, stereos, VCRs, video games, etc.)

DIVISION
Permanent

AWARD
Gold

TITLE
Nintendo Game Boy Color Hanging Factice

CLIENT
Nintendo of America

ENTRANT
JP Marketing Services
Santa Fe Springs, CA

SUB-CATEGORY
Home Entertainment - Non-Interactive, Non-
Motion or Non-Illuminated (including radios,
TVs, stereos, VCRs, video games, etc.)

DIVISION
Semi-Permanent

AWARD
Gold

TITLE
Pentium III Launch POP Campaign

CLIENT
Intel Corporation

ENTRANT
Rapid Displays
Union City, CA

SUB-CATEGORY
Computer Hardware

DIVISION
Semi-Permanent

AWARD
Gold

TITLE
Prince Of Egypt Floor Display

CLIENT
Dreamworks, SKG Home
Entertainment

ENTRANT
Origin, LLC
Burbank, CA

SUB-CATEGORY
Movies, Tapes, Records, CDs

DIVISION
Temporary

AWARD
Gold

TITLE
Rugrats 60pc Mixed Product
Merchandiser

CLIENT
Paramount Pictures Home Video

ENTRANT
Chesapeake Display & Packaging
Winston Salem, NC

SUB-CATEGORY
Movies, Tapes, Records, CDs

DIVISION
Temporary

AWARD
Silver

TITLE
PowerDeck Floor Merchandiser

CLIENT
The Upper Deck Company, L.L.C.

ENTRANT
R/P Creative Sales, Inc.
Burbank, CA

SUB-CATEGORY
Computer Software

DIVISION
Permanent

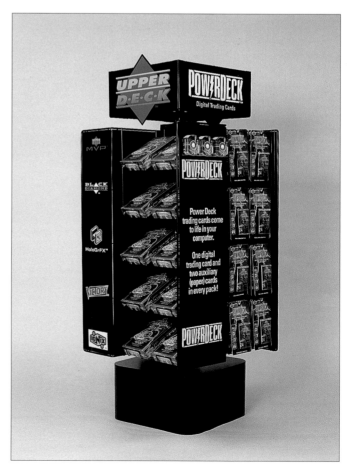

AWARD
Silver

TITLE
Display Program-Nintendo 64
& Game Boy Color

CLIENT
Nintendo of America, Inc.

ENTRANT
Design Phase, Inc.
Northbrook, IL

SUB-CATEGORY
Home Entertainment - Interactive,
Motion or Illuminated (including radios,
TVs, stereos, VCRs, video games, etc.)

DIVISION
Permanent

AWARD
Silver

TITLE
Video Game Cabinet

CLIENT
Nintendo of America Inc.

ENTRANT
Frank Mayer & Associates, Inc.
Grafton, WI

SUB-CATEGORY
Home Entertainment - Non-Interactive, Non-
Motion or Non-Illuminated (including radios,
TVs, stereos, VCRs, video games, etc.)

DIVISION
Permanent

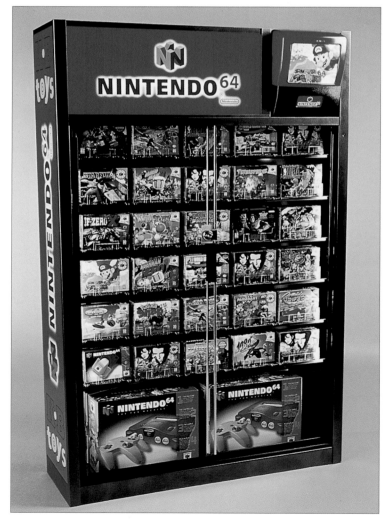

AWARD
Silver

TITLE
Palm Computing Staples Endcap

CLIENT
3Com Palm Computing, Inc.

ENTRANT
Rapid Displays
Union City, CA

SUB-CATEGORY
Computer Hardware

DIVISION
Semi-Permanent

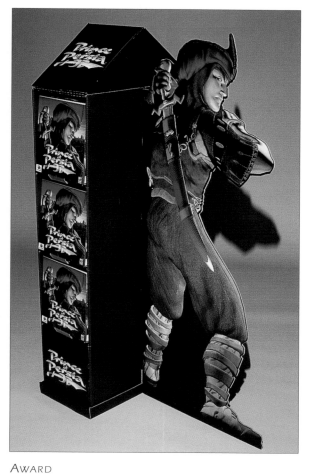

AWARD
Silver

TITLE
Prince of Persia 24-Pack Floor Display

CLIENT
Mindscape

ENTRANT
Allpak Container
Renton, WA

SUB-CATEGORY
Computer Software

DIVISION
Semi-Permanent

AWARD
Silver

TITLE
Donkey Kong 64 Standee

CLIENT
Nintendo of America

ENTRANT
The Corporate Image
Seattle, WA

SUB-CATEGORY
Home Entertainment - Non-
Interactive, Non-Motion or
Non-Illuminated (including radios,
TVs, stereos, VCRs, video games, etc.)

DIVISION
Semi-Permanent

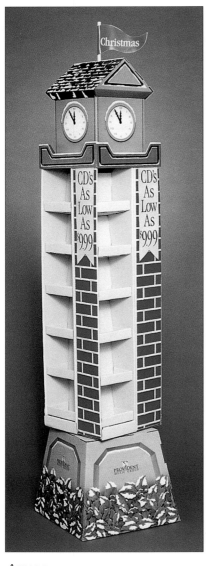

AWARD
Silver

TITLE
Provident Christmas Clock
Tower

CLIENT
Provident Music Distribution,
Brian Mitchell

ENTRANT
E and E Display Group
Lawrence, KS

SUB-CATEGORY
Movies, Tapes, Records, CDs

DIVISION
Semi-Permanent

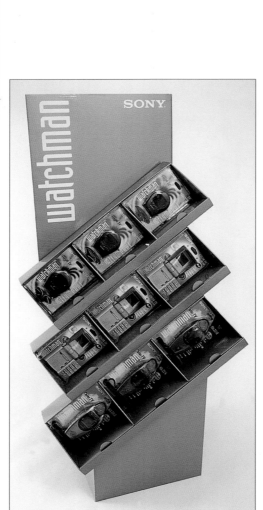

AWARD
Silver

TITLE
Resident Evil 3:
Nemesis Standee

CLIENT
CapCom

ENTRANT
Phoenix Display/
International Paper
Thorofare, NJ

SUB-CATEGORY
Computer Software

DIVISION
Temporary

AWARD
Silver

TITLE
Sony Watchman Display

CLIENT
Sony Electronics Corporation

ENTRANT
Smurfit-Stone Display Group
Carol Stream, IL

SUB-CATEGORY
Home Entertainment - Non-Interactive,
Non-Motion or Non-Illuminated
(including radios, TVs, stereos, VCRs, video games, etc.)

DIVISION
Temporary

AWARD
Silver

TITLE
The Mummy 48pc Floor Merchandiser

CLIENT
Universal Studios Home Video

ENTRANT
Chesapeake Display & Packaging
Winston Salem, NC

SUB-CATEGORY
Movies, Tapes, Records, CDs

DIVISION
Temporary

AWARD
Silver

TITLE
Madeline Lost In Paris
Half Stack Merchadiser

CLIENT
Buena Vista Home
Entertainment

ENTRANT
Cornerstone Display Group, Inc.
San Fernando, CA

SUB-CATEGORY
Movies, Tapes, Records, CDs

DIVISION
Temporary

AWARD
Silver

TITLE
My Favorite Martian

CLIENT
Buena Vista Home
Entertainment

ENTRANT
Smurfit-Stone Display Group
Carol Stream, IL

SUB-CATEGORY
Movies, Tapes, Records, CDs

DIVISION
Temporary

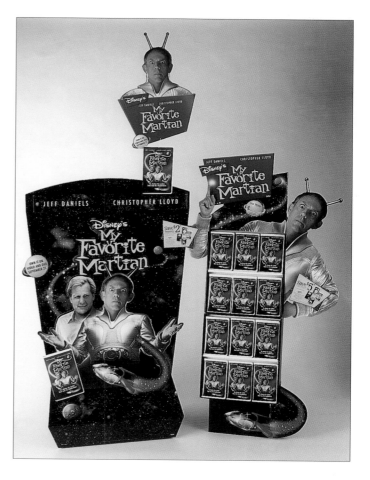

AWARD
Bronze

TITLE
Anypoint Home Network Endcap

CLIENT
Intel Corporation

ENTRANT
Frank Mayer & Associates, Inc.
Grafton, WI

SUB-CATEGORY
Computer Hardware

DIVISION
Permanent

AWARD
Bronze

TITLE
Office Depot/Sears Inline Aisle System

CLIENT
Intel Corporation

ENTRANT
Frank Mayer & Associates, Inc.
Grafton, WI

SUB-CATEGORY
Computer Hardware

DIVISION
Permanent

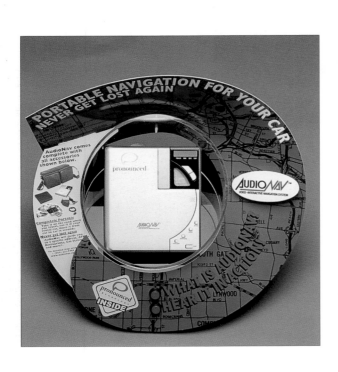

AWARD
Bronze

TITLE
Audio Nav Voice Interactive Navigation
System

CLIENT
Pronounced Technologies

ENTRANT
Packaging Corp. Of America
South Gate, CA

SUB-CATEGORY
Computer Hardware

DIVISION
Permanent

AWARD
Bronze

TITLE
Comp USA Floor Display

CLIENT
Symantec Corporation

ENTRANT
Rapid Displays
Union City, CA

SUB-CATEGORY
Computer Software

DIVISION
Permanent

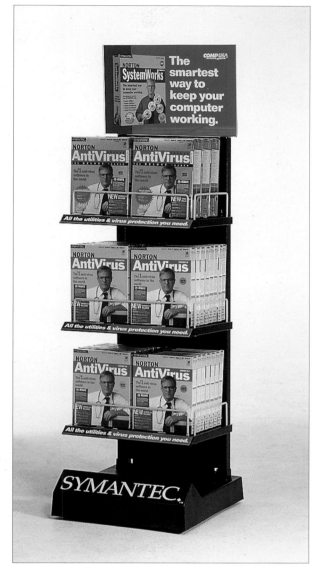

AWARD
Bronze

TITLE
Pokemon SNAP Station

CLIENT
Nintendo of America Inc.

ENTRANT
Frank Mayer & Associates, Inc.
Grafton, WI

SUB-CATEGORY
Home Entertainment - Interactive,
Motion or Illuminated
(including radios, TVs, stereos,
VCRs, video games, etc.)

DIVISION
Permanent

AWARD
Bronze

TITLE
Microsoft IntelliMouse Display

CLIENT
Microsoft Corporation

ENTRANT
Gage In-Store Marketing
Minneapolis, MN

SUB-CATEGORY
Home Entertainment - Interactive,
Motion or Illuminated
(including radios, TVs, stereos,
VCRs, video games, etc.)

DIVISION
Permanent

AWARD
Bronze

TITLE
Microsoft Game Device Display

CLIENT
Microsoft Corporation

ENTRANT
Gage In-Store Marketing
Minneapolis, MN

SUB-CATEGORY
Home Entertainment - Interactive,
Motion or Illuminated (including radios,
TVs, stereos, VCRs, video games, etc.)

DIVISION
Permanent

AWARD
Bronze

TITLE
Philips Toys 'R Us WebTV Display

CLIENT
Philips Consumer Electronics

ENTRANT
DCI Marketing
Milwaukee, WI

SUB-CATEGORY
Home Entertainment - Non-Interactive,
Non-Motion or Non-Illuminated (including
radios, TVs, stereos, VCRs, video games, etc.)

DIVISION
Permanent

AWARD
Bronze

TITLE
Pokemon Pikachu Statue

CLIENT
Nintendo of America Inc.

ENTRANT
Frank Mayer & Associates, Inc.
Grafton, WI

SUB-CATEGORY
Home Entertainment - Non-Interactive,
Non-Motion or Non-Illuminated (including
radios, TVs, stereos, VCRs, video games, etc.)

DIVISION
Permanent

AWARD
Bronze

TITLE
Top Hits Big "D" / Little "D"

CLIENT
Top Hits Music

ENTRANT
Creative Acrylics
Kenosha, WI

SUB-CATEGORY
Movies, Tapes, Records, CDs

DIVISION
Permanent

AWARD
Bronze

TITLE
Sony Monitor Side Wrap

CLIENT
Billy Shen Art Direction

ENTRANT
Rapid Displays
Union City, CA

SUB-CATEGORY
Computer Hardware

DIVISION
Semi-Permanent

AWARD
Bronze

TITLE
Starcraft Computer Software Standee

CLIENT
Havas Interactive, Inc

ENTRANT
Cornerstone Display Group, Inc.
San Fernando, CA

SUB-CATEGORY
Computer Software

DIVISION
Semi-Permanent

AWARD
Bronze

TITLE
Apple MAC OS9 Shelf Display

CLIENT
US Web / CKS

ENTRANT
Rapid Displays
Union City, CA

SUB-CATEGORY
Computer Software

DIVISION
Semi-Permanent

AWARD
Bronze

TITLE
Star Wars Racer Counter Card

CLIENT
Nintendo of America

ENTRANT
The Corporate Image
Seattle, WA

SUB-CATEGORY
Home Entertainment - Non-Interactive,
Non-Motion or Non-Illuminated (including
radios, TVs, stereos, VCRs, video games, etc.)

DIVISION
Semi-Permanent

AWARD
Bronze

TITLE
Star Wars Racer Hanging Mobile

CLIENT
Nintendo of America

ENTRANT
The Corporate Image
Seattle, WA

SUB-CATEGORY
Home Entertainment - Non-Interactive,
Non-Motion or Non-Illuminated (including
radios, TVs, stereos, VCRs, video games, etc.)

DIVISION
Semi-Permanent

AWARD
Bronze

TITLE
Now Volume 2 Two Sided Floor Display

CLIENT
EMI Music Distribution

ENTRANT
Carqueville Graphics
Canyon Country, CA

SUB-CATEGORY
Movies, Tapes, Records, CDs

DIVISION
Semi-Permanent

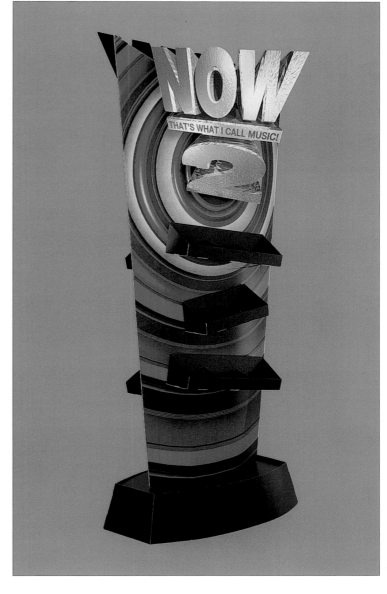

AWARD
Bronze

TITLE
1999 BMG Holiday Product Center

CLIENT
BMG Distribution

ENTRANT
Einson Freeman
Paramus, NJ

SUB-CATEGORY
Movies, Tapes, Records, CDs

DIVISION
Semi-Permanent

AWARD
Bronze

TITLE
SideWinder Demo Endcap

CLIENT
Microsoft

ENTRANT
Promo Edge Division of
Menasha Corporation
Menomonee Falls, WI

SUB-CATEGORY
Computer Hardware

DIVISION
Temporary

AWARD
Bronze

TITLE
WSJ.com

CLIENT
Wall Street Journal

ENTRANT
Inland Consumer
Packaging and Displays
Indianapolis, IN

SUB-CATEGORY
Computer Software

DIVISION
Temporary

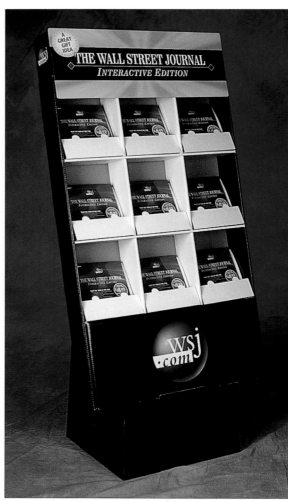

AWARD
Bronze

TITLE
Leap Ahead Floor Display

CLIENT
The Learning Company

ENTRANT
Inland Consumer Packaging
and Displays
Indianapolis, IN

SUB-CATEGORY
Computer Software

DIVISION
Temporary

AWARD
Bronze

TITLE
The Learning Company Clamshell Display

CLIENT
The Learning Company

ENTRANT
Inland Consumer Packaging and Displays
Indianapolis, IN

SUB-CATEGORY
Computer Software

DIVISION
Temporary

AWARD
Bronze

TITLE
Bugs Life Video Standee and
Prepack

CLIENT
Buena Vista Home Entertainment

ENTRANT
Cornerstone Display Group, Inc.
San Fernando, CA

SUB-CATEGORY
Movies, Tapes, Records, CDs

DIVISION
Temporary

AWARD
Bronze

TITLE
Mulan Video Standee and Mobile

CLIENT
Buena Vista Home Entertainment

ENTRANT
Cornerstone Display Group, Inc.
San Fernando, CA

SUB-CATEGORY
Movies, Tapes, Records, CDs

DIVISION
Temporary

AWARD
Bronze

TITLE
Pokemon, The First Movie

CLIENT
Warner Brothers

ENTRANT
Drissi Advertising
Los Angeles, CA

SUB-CATEGORY
Movies, Tapes, Records, CDs

DIVISION
Temporary

AWARD
Bronze

TITLE
Austin Powers:
The Spy Who Shagged Me

CLIENT
New Line Cinema

ENTRANT
Drissi Advertising
Los Angeles, CA

SUB-CATEGORY
Movies, Tapes, Records, CDs

DIVISION
Temporary

AWARD
Bronze

TITLE
007: The World is Not Enough

CLIENT
MGM

ENTRANT
Drissi Advertising
Los Angeles, CA

SUB-CATEGORY
Movies, Tapes, Records, CDs

DIVISION
Temporary

AWARD
Gold

TITLE
Estée Lauder Promotional Focus Unit

CLIENT
Estée Lauder Corporation

ENTRANT
Trans World Marketing
East Rutherford, NJ

SUB-CATEGORY
Men's and Women's Colognes,
Fragrances, Eaux de Toilette, etc.

DIVISION
Permanent

AWARD
Gold

TITLE
Estée Lauder Full Line
Fragrance Unit

CLIENT
Estée Lauder, Inc.

ENTRANT
Consumer Promotions
International
Mount Vernon, NY

SUB-CATEGORY
Women's Perfumes

DIVISION
Permanent

AWARD
Gold

TITLE
Green Tea Counter Merchandiser

CLIENT
Elizabeth Arden

ENTRANT
Trans World Marketing
East Rutherford, NJ

SUB-CATEGORY
Men's and Women's Colognes,
Fragrances, Eaux de Toilette, etc.

DIVISION
Semi-Permanent

AWARD
Gold

TITLE
Stetson Full Pallet

CLIENT
Coty

ENTRANT
Advertising Display Company
Lyndhurst, NJ

SUB-CATEGORY
Men's and Women's Colognes,
Fragrances, Eaux de Toilette, etc.

DIVISION
Temporary

AWARD
Gold

TITLE
Coty X-mas Islander Unit

CLIENT
Coty

ENTRANT
Advertising Display Company
Lyndhurst, NJ

SUB-CATEGORY
Men's and Women's Colognes,
Fragrances, Eaux de Toilette, etc.

DIVISION
Temporary

AWARD
Gold

TITLE
Parfums de Couer Juice Bar 8 Oz. Mini

CLIENT
Parfums de Couer

ENTRANT
Triangle Display Group
Philadelphia, PA

SUB-CATEGORY
Women's Perfumes

DIVISION
Temporary

AWARD
Silver

TITLE
Very Valentino Homme Displays

CLIENT
Elizabeth Arden Ltd.

ENTRANT
Consumer Promotions International
Mount Vernon, NY

SUB-CATEGORY
Men's and Women's Colognes,
Fragrances, Eaux de Toilette, etc.

DIVISION
Permanent

AWARD
Silver

TITLE
Ralph Lauren Romance
Floorstand

CLIENT
Prestige Et Collections
International

ENTRANT
Consumer Promotions
International
Mount Vernon, NY

SUB-CATEGORY
Women's Perfumes

DIVISION
Permanent

AWARD
Silver

TITLE
Holiday 1/2 and 1/4 Pallet

CLIENT
Coty

ENTRANT
**Advertising Display Company
Lyndhurst, NJ**

SUB-CATEGORY
**Men's and Women's Colognes, Fragrances,
Eaux de Toilette, etc.**

DIVISION
Temporary

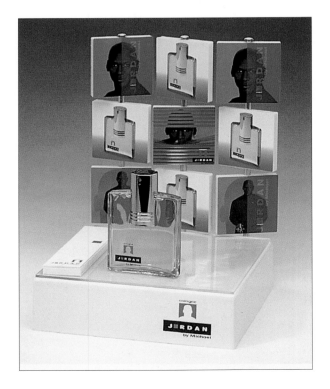

AWARD
Bronze

TITLE
**Jordan by Michael -
Tester Unit**

CLIENT
Bijan Fragrances, Inc.

ENTRANT
**JP Marketing Services
Santa Fe Springs, CA**

SUB-CATEGORY
**Men's and Women's
Colognes, Fragrances,
Eaux de Toilette, etc.**

DIVISION
Permanent

AWARD
Bronze

TITLE
DKNY Fragrance Tester Tower

CLIENT
Donna Karen Fragrances

ENTRANT
**IDMD Manufacturing Inc.
Toronto, ON, Canada**

SUB-CATEGORY
**Men's and Women's Colognes,
Fragrances, Eaux de Toilette, etc."**

DIVISION
Permanent

AWARD
Bronze

TITLE
Tommy Hilfiger Freedom
Fragrance Launch

CLIENT
Estée Lauder Corporation

ENTRANT
Trans World Marketing
East Rutherford, NJ

SUB-CATEGORY
Men's and Women's Colognes,
Fragrances, Eaux de Toilette, etc.

DIVISION
Permanent

AWARD
Bronze

TITLE
Viking Collateral (Banner,
Tablecloth, Trypt)

CLIENT
The Five Star Fragrance Company

ENTRANT
The Royal Promotion Group
New York, NY

SUB-CATEGORY
Men's and Women's Colognes,
Fragrances, Eaux de Toilette, etc.

DIVISION
Semi-Permanent

AWARD
Bronze

TITLE
Jako Tower Display

CLIENT
Elizabeth Arden

ENTRANT
Taurus Packaging
Cherry Hill, NJ

SUB-CATEGORY
Men's and Women's Colognes,
Fragrances, Eaux de Toilette, etc.

DIVISION
Temporary

AWARD
Gold

TITLE
Planters 27 Case Baking Easel

CLIENT
Nabisco Foods Company - Planters Division

ENTRANT
Oxford Innovations, Div. Of Tim-Bar Corp.
New Oxford, PA

SUB-CATEGORY
Frozen, Fresh and Refrigerated Foods (including seafood, baked goods, produce, dairy, meats, etc.)

DIVISION
Semi-Permanent

AWARD
Gold

TITLE
Bakery Four Shelf Display

CLIENT
Pepperidge Farm

ENTRANT
Smurfit-Stone Display Group
Richmond, VA

SUB-CATEGORY
Containerized and
Processed Foods
(including coffee, tea, canned,
concentrated and fresh juices, etc.)

DIVISION
Temporary

AWARD
Gold

TITLE
Les Poochs Brush Display

CLIENT
Les Poochs

ENTRANT
Promotional Development Inc.
Brooklyn, NY

SUB-CATEGORY
Pet Food and Accessories
(including canned food, bag food, flea
collars, sprays, baths, pet toys, leashes, etc.)

DIVISION
Permanent

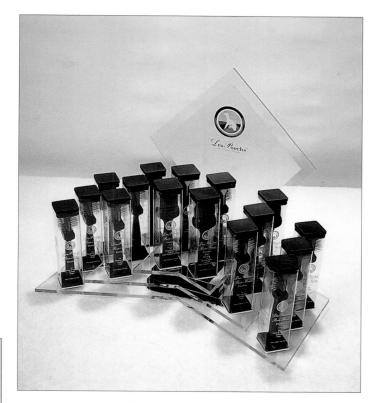

AWARD
Silver

TITLE
Starbucks Modular Merchandiser

CLIENT
Kraftfoods

ENTRANT
Henschel-Steinau, Inc.
Englewood, NJ

SUB-CATEGORY
Containerized and Processed Foods
(including coffee, tea, canned,
concentrated and fresh juices, etc.)

DIVISION
Permanent

AWARD
Silver

TITLE
Doughboy Celebration Display

CLIENT
The Pillsbury Company

ENTRANT
Promo Edge Division
of Menasha Corporation
Menomonee Falls, WI

SUB-CATEGORY
Containerized and
Processed Foods
(including coffee, tea, canned,
concentrated and fresh juices, etc.)

DIVISION
Semi-Permanent

SILVER
Texas Farm Products

CLIENT
Texas Farm Products

ENTRANT
Longview Fibre Display
Group
Milwaukee, WI

SUB-CATEGORY
Paper Goods and Soap

DIVISION
Semi-Permanent

AWARD
Silver

TITLE
Kellogg Special K Plus Prepack

CLIENT
Kellogg USA Girard and Gausselin

ENTRANT
E and E Display Group
Lawrence, KS

SUB-CATEGORY
Containerized and
Processed Foods
(including coffee, tea, canned,
concentrated and fresh juices, etc.)

DIVISION
Temporary

AWARD
Bronze

TITLE
Home Meal Solutions Rolling Rack

CLIENT
Nabisco Foods Company

ENTRANT
ImageWorks Display & Marketing
Group
Winston Salem, NC

SUB-CATEGORY
Containerized and Processed Foods
(including coffee, tea, canned,
concentrated and fresh juices, etc.)

DIVISION
Permanent

AWARD
Silver

TITLE
Pacific Gardens floorstand

CLIENT
Dugan Valva Contess

ENTRANT
Thomson-Leeds Company Inc.
Sunnyside, NY

SUB-CATEGORY
Paper Goods and Soap

DIVISION
Temporary

AWARD
Bronze

TITLE
Oatmeal Express Counter
Merchandiser

CLIENT
The Quaker Oats Company

ENTRANT
United Displaycraft
Des Plaines, IL

SUB-CATEGORY
Containerized and Processed Foods
(including coffee, tea, canned,
concentrated and fresh juices, etc.)

DIVISION
Permanent

AWARD
Bronze

TITLE
Kingsford BBQ Center Pavilion

CLIENT
Clorox Company

ENTRANT
Rapid Displays
Union City, CA

SUB-CATEGORY
Paper Goods and Soap

DIVISION
Semi-Permanent

AWARD
Bronze

TITLE
JELL-O 20 Case Floorstand

CLIENT
Madden Communications, Inc.

ENTRANT
Inland Consumer Packaging
and Displays
Indianapolis, IN

SUB-CATEGORY
Containerized and Processed
Foods (including coffee,
tea, canned, concentrated
and fresh juices, etc.)

DIVISION
Temporary

AWARD
Bronze

TITLE
Kellogg's K-sential Tower Display

CLIENT
Garner & Nevins Marketing

ENTRANT
C.D. Baird & Co., Inc.
West Allis, WI

SUB-CATEGORY
Containerized and Processed Foods
(including coffee, tea, canned, concentrated and fresh juices, etc.)

DIVISION
Temporary

AWARD
Bronze

TITLE
Cellasene Display

CLIENT
Rexall Sundown

ENTRANT
Inland Consumer Packaging and Displays
Indianapolis, IN

SUB-CATEGORY
Paper Goods and Soap

DIVISION
Temporary

AWARD
Bronze

TITLE
Big Book Floor Display

CLIENT
Schmidt-Cannon

ENTRANT
One Source Industries, LLC.
Laguna Hills, CA

SUB-CATEGORY
Paper Goods and Soap

DIVISION
Temporary

AWARD
Bronze

TITLE
Texas Farm Products 5 SKU Tray

CLIENT
Texas Farm Products

ENTRANT
Longview Fibre DisplayGroup
Milwaukee, WI

SUB-CATEGORY
Pet Food and Accessories (including
canned food, bag food, flea collars,
sprays, baths, pet toys, leashes, etc.)

DIVISION
Temporary

AWARD
Gold

TITLE
Estée Lauder Sun Tester

CLIENT
Estée Lauder Inc.

ENTRANT
IDMD Manufacturing Inc.
Toronto, ON, Canada

SUB-CATEGORY
Suntan Products, Lotions,
Moisturizers, and Creams

DIVISION
Permanent

AWARD
Gold

TITLE
Candy Kisses Mini-Compact Tray

CLIENT
Beautycology, Inc.

ENTRANT
Triangle Display Group
Philadelphia, PA

SUB-CATEGORY
Skin Care Products (including cleansers,
shaving creams, aftershaves, etc.)

DIVISION
Semi-Permanent

AWARD
Gold

TITLE
Heart Candy Kisses Counter Display

CLIENT
Beautycology, Inc.

ENTRANT
Triangle Display Group
Philadelphia, PA

SUB-CATEGORY
Skin Care Products (including cleansers,
shaving creams, aftershaves, etc.)

DIVISION
Semi-Permanent

AWARD
Gold

TITLE
Johnson's Kid Floorstand/
Powerwing

CLIENT
Johnson & Johnson Consumer
Products Inc.

ENTRANT
Smurfit-Stone Display Group
Richmond, VA

SUB-CATEGORY
Hair Cleansing Treatments (including
shampoos and conditioners, etc.)

DIVISION
Temporary

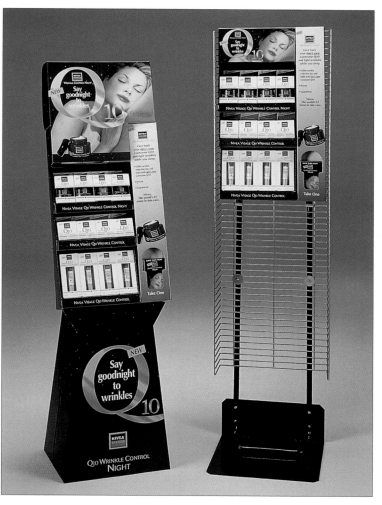

AWARD
Gold

TITLE
Beiersdorf Q-10 Night
Powerwing/Floorstand

CLIENT
Beiersdorf Inc.

ENTRANT
Triangle Display Group
Philadelphia, PA

SUB-CATEGORY
Suntan Products, Lotions,
Moisturizers, and Creams

DIVISION
Temporary

AWARD
Silver

TITLE
Rusk/Deep Shine Glorifier

CLIENT
Rusk, Inc.

ENTRANT
Henschel-Steinau, Inc.
Englewood, NJ

SUB-CATEGORY
Hair Cleansing Treatments
(including shampoos and conditioners, etc.)

DIVISION
Permanent

AWARD
Silver

TITLE
Ponds Clear Solutions SK/FS

CLIENT
Unilever HPC - USA

ENTRANT
Advertising Display Company
Lyndhurst, NJ

SUB-CATEGORY
Skin Care Products
(including cleansers, shaving
creams, aftershaves, etc.)

DIVISION
Semi-Permanent

AWARD
Silver

TITLE
Thierry Mugler Skincare General Tester Stand

CLIENT
Thierry Mugler

ENTRANT
Diam Groupe
Les Mureaux, Cedex, France

SUB-CATEGORY
Skin Care Products (including cleansers, shaving creams, aftershaves, etc.)

DIVISION
Permanent

AWARD
Silver

TITLE
Coppertone Spray Custom Powerwing

CLIENT
Schering-Plough Healthcare Products

ENTRANT
Mechtronics Corporation
Stamford, CT

SUB-CATEGORY
Suntan Products, Lotions, Moisturizers, and Creams

DIVISION
Semi-Permanent

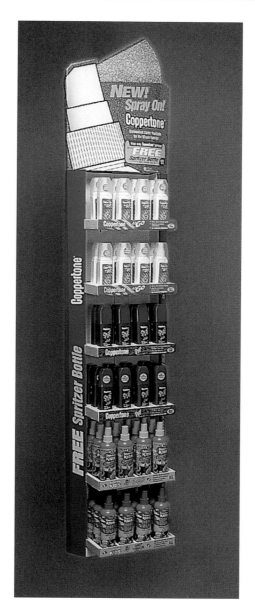

AWARD
Silver

TITLE
Wahl/Walmart Gift Box Half Pallet

CLIENT
Wahl Clipper Corporation

ENTRANT
Longview Fibre DisplayGroup
Milwaukee, WI

SUB-CATEGORY
Brushes, Hairdryers, Razors, and Combs

DIVISION
Temporary

AWARD
Silver

TITLE
Pantene Pro-V Ultra-V 60's Floorstand

CLIENT
Procter & Gamble Company

ENTRANT
Chesapeake Display & Packaging
Winston Salem, NC

SUB-CATEGORY
Hair Cleansing Treatments (including shampoos and conditioners, etc.)

DIVISION
Temporary

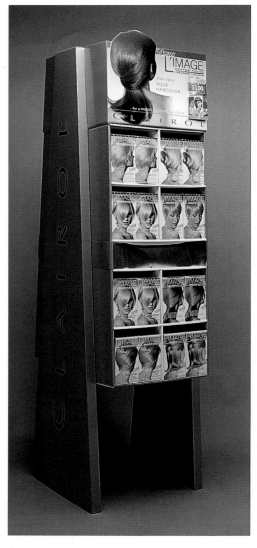

AWARD
Silver

TITLE
L'Image Combo Floor Display

CLIENT
Bristol Myers Squibb

ENTRANT
Techno P.O.S. inc.
Anjou, PQ, Canada

SUB-CATEGORY
Hair Styling and Coloring Products
(including mousse, gels, etc.)

DIVISION
Temporary

AWARD
Silver

TITLE
Line Eraser Multifunctional Display

CLIENT
Cosmair

ENTRANT
Techno P.O.S. inc.
Anjou, PQ, Canada

SUB-CATEGORY
Suntan Products, Lotions,
Moisturizers, and Creams

DIVISION
Temporary

AWARD
Silver

TITLE
Noxzema Skin Fitness Cleansing SK/FS

CLIENT
Procter & Gamble Company

ENTRANT
Chesapeake Display & Packaging
Winston Salem, NC

SUB-CATEGORY
Suntan Products, Lotions, Moisturizers,
and Creams

DIVISION
Temporary

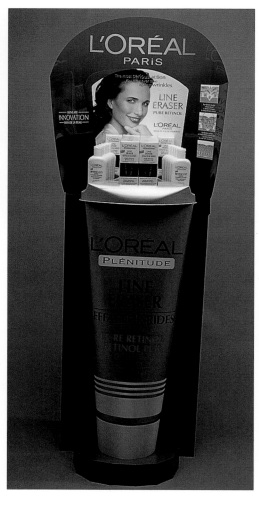

AWARD
Bronze

TITLE
Nioxin Floorstand

CLIENT
Nioxin Research Lab's

ENTRANT
P.O.P. Displays International
Woodside, NY

SUB-CATEGORY
Hair Cleansing Treatments
(including shampoos and
conditioners, etc.)

DIVISION
Permanent

AWARD
Bronze

TITLE
Matrix Amplify Lighted Display

CLIENT
Matrix Essentials

ENTRANT
Promotional Developmet Inc.
Brooklyn, NY

SUB-CATEGORY
Hair Cleansing Treatments
(including shampoos and
conditioners, etc.)

DIVISION
Permanent

AWARD
Bronze

TITLE
New Ultress Custom Colour
Premium Display

CLIENT
Clairol

ENTRANT
Markson Rosenthal & Company
Englewood Cliffs, NJ

SUB-CATEGORY
Hair Styling and Coloring Products
(including mousse, gels, etc.)

DIVISION
Permanent

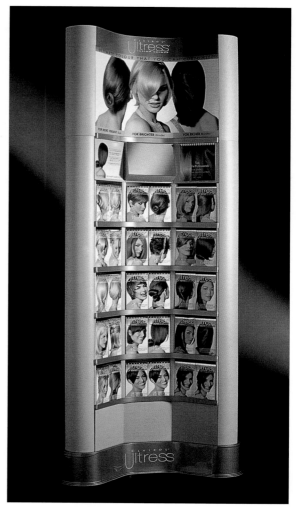

AWARD
Bronze

TITLE
Estée Lauder "Re-Nutriv" Counter Display

CLIENT
Estée Lauder, Inc.

ENTRANT
**Consumer Promotions International
Mount Vernon, NY**

SUB-CATEGORY
**Skin Care Products (including cleansers,
shaving creams, aftershaves, etc.)**

DIVISION
Permanent

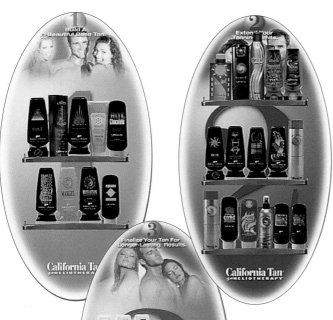

AWARD
Bronze

TITLE
**California Suncare Mega-
Mix Wall Display Syst**

CLIENT
California Suncare

ENTRANT
**JP Marketing Services
Santa Fe Springs, CA**

SUB-CATEGORY
**Suntan Products, Lotions,
Moisturizers, and Creams**

DIVISION
Permanent

AWARD
Bronze

TITLE
Nature's Accents Merch. System For K-Mart

CLIENT
The Dial Corporation

ENTRANT
**The Niven Marketing Group
Bensenville, IL**

SUB-CATEGORY
**Skin Care Products (including cleansers,
shaving creams, aftershaves, etc.)**

DIVISION
Permanent

AWARD
Bronze

TITLE
SensorCare Hair Dryer/Clipper
Display

CLIENT
Norelco

ENTRANT
Frank Mayer & Associates, Inc.
Grafton, WI

SUB-CATEGORY
Brushes, Hairdryers, Razors, and
Combs

DIVISION
Semi-Permanent

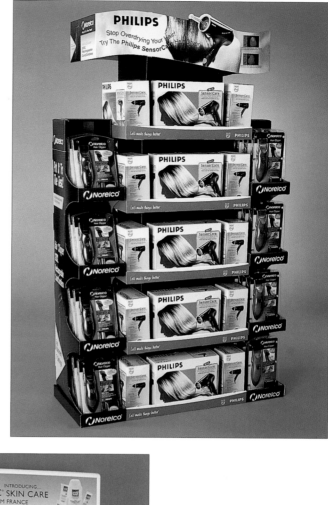

AWARD
Bronze

TITLE
Dove Nutrium 12oz. S.K./ F.S>

CLIENT
Unilever HPC - USA

ENTRANT
Advertising Display Company
Lyndhurst, NJ

SUB-CATEGORY
Skin Care Products
(including cleansers, shaving
creams, aftershaves, etc.)

DIVISION
Semi-Permanent

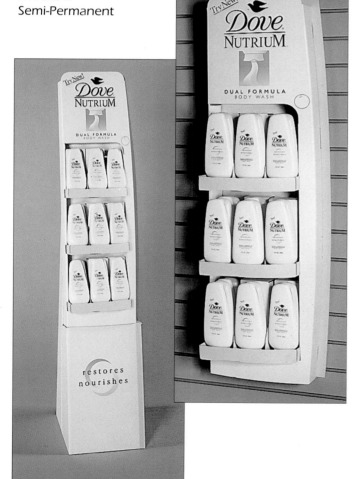

AWARD
Bronze

TITLE
"Roc" Powerwing

CLIENT
Johnson and Johnson
Consumer Product Co.

ENTRANT
Henschel-Steinau, Inc.
Englewood, NJ

SUB-CATEGORY
Suntan Products, Lotions,
Moisturizers, and Creams

DIVISION
Semi-Permanent

AWARD
Bronze

TITLE
Sarah Michaels Wal*Mart Pallet Display

CLIENT
The Dial Corporation

ENTRANT
Smyth Companies - Display Division
Saint Paul, MN

SUB-CATEGORY
Suntan Products, Lotions, Moisturizers, and Creams

DIVISION
Semi-Permanent

AWARD
Bronze

TITLE
Baby Gel Multifunctional Display

CLIENT
Johnson & Johnson

ENTRANT
Techno P.O.S. Inc.
Anjou, PQ, Canada

SUB-CATEGORY
Hair Cleansing Treatments (including
shampoos and conditioners, etc.)

DIVISION
Temporary

AWARD
Bronze

TITLE
Nutrisse Floor Display

CLIENT
Cosmair

ENTRANT
Techno P.O.S. inc.
Anjou, PQ, Canada

SUB-CATEGORY
Hair Styling and
Coloring Products
(including mousse, gels, etc.)

DIVISION
Temporary

AWARD
Bronze

TITLE
Nivea Skin Firming Lotion PW/FS

CLIENT
Beiersdorf

ENTRANT
**Rand Display, Inc.
Teaneck, NJ**

SUB-CATEGORY
**Skin Care Products (including cleansers,
shaving creams, aftershaves, etc.)**

DIVISION
Temporary

AWARD
Bronze

TITLE
Clean and Clear Floor Display

CLIENT
Johnson & Johnson

ENTRANT
**Techno P.O.S. inc.
Anjou, PQ, Canada**

SUB-CATEGORY
**Skin Care Products (including cleansers,
shaving creams, aftershaves, etc.)**

DIVISION
Temporary

AWARD
Bronze

TITLE
Turning Point Multi-Use Display

CLIENT
L'Oréal Canada

ENTRANT
**Point 1 Displays Inc.
Montreal, Quebec, Canada**

SUB-CATEGORY
**Skin Care Products
(including cleansers, shaving
creams, aftershaves, etc.)**

DIVISION
Temporary

AWARD
Bronze

TITLE
Noxzema Skin Fitness Moisturizer SK/FS

CLIENT
Procter & Gamble Company

ENTRANT
Chesapeake Display & Packaging
Winston Salem, NC

SUB-CATEGORY
Suntan Products, Lotions,
Moisturizers, and Creams

DIVISION
Temporary

AWARD
Bronze

TITLE
Eucerin Universal
Powerwing/Floorstand

CLIENT
Beiersdorf, Inc.

ENTRANT
Triangle Display Group
Philadelphia, PA

SUB-CATEGORY
Suntan Products, Lotions,
Moisturizers, and Creams

DIVISION
Temporary

AWARD
Bronze

TITLE
Eucerin 16 Oz., 18 Pc.
Powerwing/Floorstand

CLIENT
Beiersdorf, Inc.

ENTRANT
Triangle Display Group
Philadelphia, PA

SUB-CATEGORY
Suntan Products, Lotions,
Moisturizers, and Creams

DIVISION
Temporary

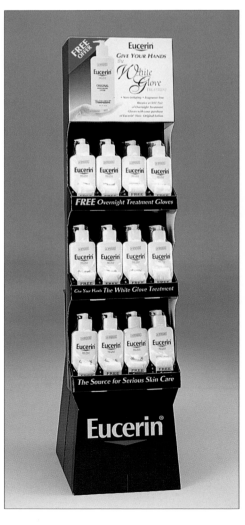

AWARD
Gold

TITLE
Whitehall-Robins Sam's Club Pallet Displays

CLIENT
Whitehall-Robins

ENTRANT
New Dimensions Research Corporation
Melville, NY

SUB-CATEGORY
First Aid and Pharmaceuticals (including analgesics,
vitamins, cough and cold remedies, etc.)

DIVISION
Permanent

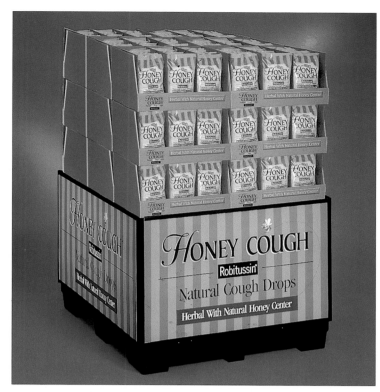

AWARD
Gold

TITLE
TheraPatch® Anti-Itch Kids 24 Ct. Display

CLIENT
LecTec Corporation

ENTRANT
Smyth Companies - Display Division
Saint Paul, MN

SUB-CATEGORY
First Aid and Pharmaceuticals
(including analgesics, vitamins, cough
and cold remedies, etc.)

DIVISION
Semi-Permanent

AWARD
Gold

TITLE
Colgate Indy Car Display

CLIENT
Busch Creative/ Colgate Palmolive

ENTRANT
Rapid Displays
Chicago, IL

SUB-CATEGORY
Dentifrices, Mouthwash and Oral Care Implements

DIVISION
Temporary

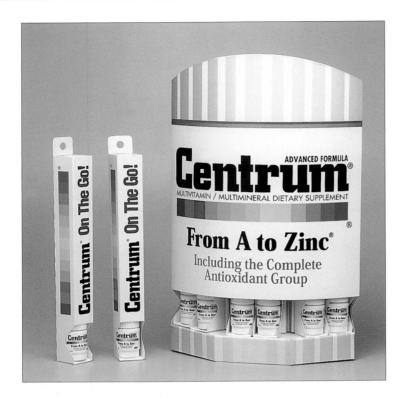

AWARD
Gold

TITLE
Centrum Bottle Gravity Feed

CLIENT
Whitehall Robins

ENTRANT
Smurfit-Stone Display Group
Richmond, VA

SUB-CATEGORY
First Aid and Pharmaceuticals
(including analgesics, vitamins,
cough and cold remedies, etc.)

DIVISION
Temporary

AWARD
Silver

TITLE
Tylenol Kmart Powerwing

CLIENT
McNeil Consumer Healthcare

ENTRANT
Mechtronics Corporation
Stamford, CT

SUB-CATEGORY
First Aid and Pharmaceuticals
(including analgesics, vitamins,
cough and cold remedies, etc.)

DIVISION
Permanent

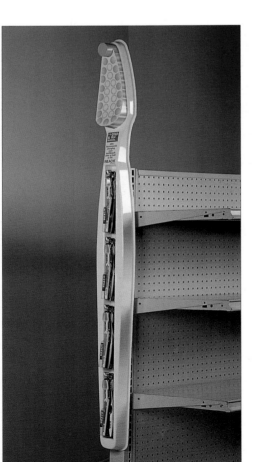

AWARD
Silver

TITLE
Reach HEB Cough & Cold

CLIENT
Johnson & Johnson PPC

ENTRANT
Resources Inc. In Display
Cranford, NJ

SUB-CATEGORY
Dentifrices, Mouthwash and
Oral Care Implements

DIVISION
Semi-Permanent

WARD
Silver

TITLE
Johnson & Johnson Fist Aid
To Go Showcase

CLIENT
Johnson & Johnson CPI

ENTRANT
Resources Inc. In Display
Cranford, NJ

SUB-CATEGORY
First Aid and Pharmaceuticals
(including analgesics, vitamins,
cough and cold remedies, etc.)

DIVISION
Semi-Permanent

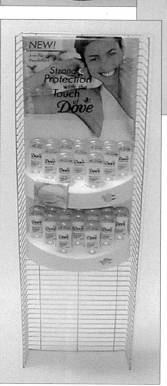

WARD
Silver

TITLE
Dove Powerwing, Mini .
Powerwing & Floorstand

CLIENT
Unilever HPC

ENTRANT
The Royal Promotion Group
New York, NY

SUB-CATEGORY
Personal Hygiene, Diapers
and Baby Care Items

DIVISION
Semi-Permanent

AWARD
Silver

TITLE
Aquafresh Flex Tip FS/SK

CLIENT
SmithKline Beecham

ENTRANT
Advertising Display
Company
Lyndhurst, NJ

SUB-CATEGORY
Dentifrices, Mouthwash
and Oral Care Implements

DIVISION
Temporary

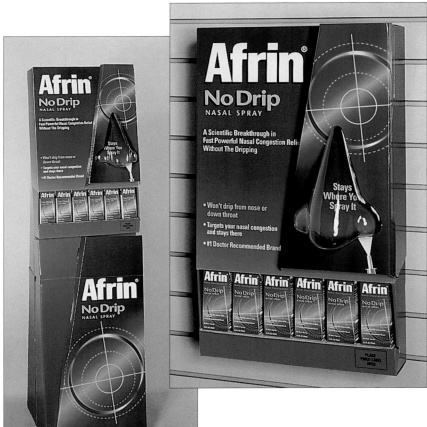

AWARD
Silver

TITLE
Afrin No Drip 24pce. FS/PW

CLIENT
Schering Plough Health Care Products

ENTRANT
Advertising Display Company
Lyndhurst, NJ

SUB-CATEGORY
First Aid and Pharmaceuticals (including analgesics, vitamins, cough and cold remedies, etc.)

DIVISION
Temporary

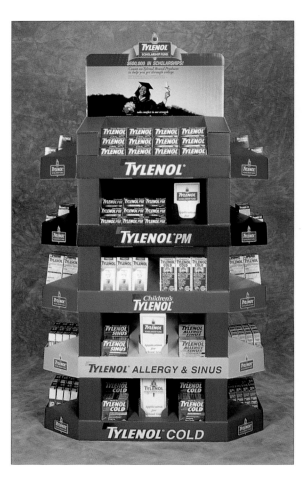

AWARD
Silver

TITLE
McNeil/Tylenol Eckerd
"Scholarship Prepack"

CLIENT
McNeil Consumer Healthcare

ENTRANT
Phoenix Display/International
Paper
Thorofare, NJ

SUB-CATEGORY
First Aid and Pharmaceuticals
(including analgesics, vitamins,
cough and cold remedies, etc.)

DIVISION
Temporary

AWARD
Silver

TITLE
Tylenol Combo Floor Display

CLIENT
McNeil Consumer Healthcare

ENTRANT
Techno P.O.S. inc.
Anjou, PQ, Canada

SUB-CATEGORY
First Aid and Pharmaceuticals
(including analgesics, vitamins,
cough and cold remedies, etc.)

DIVISION
Temporary

AWARD
Silver

TITLE
Speed Stick Clear Anti-Perspirant
Floorstand

CLIENT
Colgate-Palmolive Company

ENTRANT
Markson Rosenthal & Company
Englewood Cliffs, NJ

SUB-CATEGORY
Personal Hygiene, Diapers
and Baby Care Items

DIVISION
Temporary

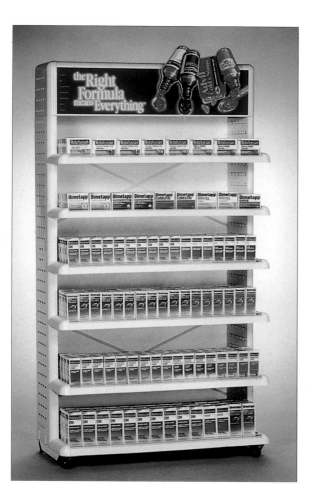

AWARD
Bronze

TITLE
Cough/Cold Floor Display

CLIENT
Whitehall-Robins

ENTRANT
Henschel-Steinau, Inc.
Englewood, NJ

SUB-CATEGORY
First Aid and Pharmaceuticals
(including analgesics, vitamins,
cough and cold remedies, etc.)

DIVISION
Permanent

AWARD
Bronze

TITLE
Leiner Tree Of Life

CLIENT
Leiner

ENTRANT
HMG Worldwide
New York, NY

SUB-CATEGORY
First Aid and Pharmaceuticals
(including analgesics, vitamins,
cough and cold remedies, etc.)

DIVISION
Permanent

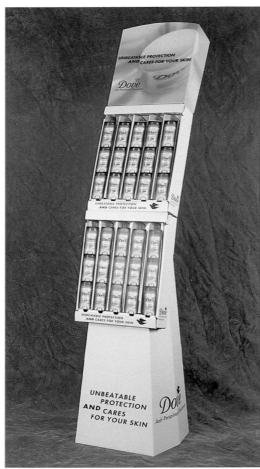

AWARD
Bronze

TITLE
Dove Antiperspirant Gravity Feed Floorstand

CLIENT
Unilever Home and Personal Care USA

ENTRANT
Phoenix Display/International Paper
Thorofare, NJ

SUB-CATEGORY
Personal Hygiene, Diapers and Baby Care Items

DIVISION
Semi-Permanent

AWARD
Bronze

TITLE
"Reach Plaque Sweeper
Between" Floorstand/PW

CLIENT
Personal Products Company

ENTRANT
Smurfit-Stone Display Group
Carol Stream, IL

SUB-CATEGORY
Dentifrices, Mouthwash and
Oral Care Implements

DIVISION
Temporary

AWARD
Bronze

TITLE
Mentadent Surround
Toothbrush Program

CLIENT
Unilever Home and
Personal Care - USA

ENTRANT
Mechtronics Corporation
Stamford, CT

SUB-CATEGORY
Dentifrices, Mouthwash and
Oral Care Implements

DIVISION
Temporary

AWARD
Bronze

TITLE
Reach "Arthur" Toothbrush
FS/PW/PDQ Tray

CLIENT
Personal Products Company

ENTRANT
Smurfit-Stone Display Group
Carol Stream, IL

SUB-CATEGORY
Dentifrices, Mouthwash and
Oral Care Implements

DIVISION
Temporary

AWARD
Bronze

TITLE
Theragran Heart Right 24 Pc.

CLIENT
Bristol-Myers Products

ENTRANT
Phoenix Display/International Paper
Thorofare, NJ

SUB-CATEGORY
First Aid and Pharmaceuticals
(including analgesics, vitamins,
cough and cold remedies, etc.)

DIVISION
Temporary

AWARD
Bronze

TITLE
Health Pac Floor Display

CLIENT
Sac Sante Inc.

ENTRANT
Point 1 Displays Inc.
Montreal, Quebec, Canada

SUB-CATEGORY
First Aid and Pharmaceuticals
(including analgesics, vitamins, cough
and cold remedies, etc.)

DIVISION
Temporary

AWARD
Bronze

TITLE
Band-Aid Brand Cushions for
Feet Floorstand

CLIENT
Johnson & Johnson Consumer
Products Inc.

ENTRANT
Smurfit-Stone Display Group
Carol Stream, IL

SUB-CATEGORY
First Aid and Pharmaceuticals
(including analgesics, vitamins,
cough and cold remedies, etc.)

DIVISION
Temporary

AWARD
Bronze

TITLE
Centrum Performance F/S

CLIENT
Whitehall Robins

ENTRANT
Smurfit-Stone Display Group
Richmond, VA

SUB-CATEGORY
First Aid and Pharmaceuticals
(including analgesics, vitamins,
cough and cold remedies, etc.)

DIVISION
Temporary

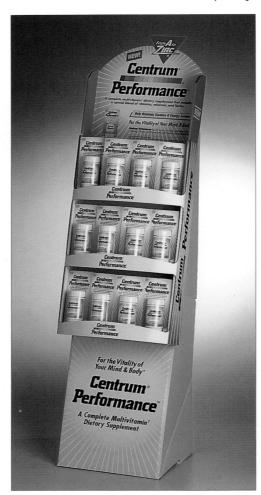

AWARD
Bronze

TITLE
Centrum Kids With
Shamu Stamper

CLIENT
Whitehall Robins

ENTRANT
Smurfit-Stone Display Group
Richmond, VA

SUB-CATEGORY
First Aid and Pharmaceuticals
(including analgesics, vitamins,
cough and cold remedies, etc.)

DIVISION
Temporary

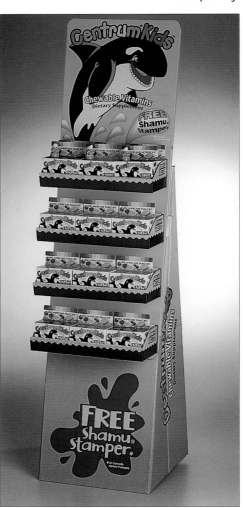

AWARD
Bronze

TITLE
Provon Floorstand

CLIENT
Gojo Industries

ENTRANT
Phoenix Display/
International Paper
Thorofare, NJ

SUB-CATEGORY
Personal Hygiene, Diapers
and Baby Care Items

DIVISION
Temporary

AWARD
Bronze

TITLE
Johnson's Safety Swabs
Floorstand/Powerwing

CLIENT
Johnson & Johnson
Consumer Products Inc.

ENTRANT
Smurfit-Stone Display Group
Carol Stream, IL

SUB-CATEGORY
Personal Hygiene, Diapers
and Baby Care Items

DIVISION
Temporary

AWARD
Bronze

TITLE
Ultra Multi Pack Family

CLIENT
Procter and Gamble Co.

ENTRANT
Smurfit-Stone Display Group
Richmond, VA

SUB-CATEGORY
Personal Hygiene, Diapers
and Baby Care Items

DIVISION
Temporary

AWARD
Gold

TITLE
Brita Faucet Filter Counter Unit

CLIENT
Brita

ENTRANT
Advertising Display Company
Lyndhurst, NJ

SUB-CATEGORY
Home Furnishings and Housewares
(including household furniture, upholstery, carpeting,
wall and floor covering, fireplace accessories, patio and
lawn furnishings, linens, kitchen needs, towels, etc.)

DIVISION
Permanent

AWARD
Gold

TITLE
MTD Yard-Man Lawn Mower
Display

CLIENT
MTD Products

ENTRANT
Cormark
Elk Grove Village, IL

SUB-CATEGORY
Lawn and Garden Supplies
(including mowers, fertilizers,
seeds, spreaders, shovels,
insecticides, pesticides, etc.)

DIVISION
Permanent

AWARD
Gold

TITLE
Kenmore Refrigerator Animator

CLIENT
ARS Advertising

ENTRANT
Creative Solutions Group
Fairfield, NJ

SUB-CATEGORY
Appliances (large and small)

DIVISION
Semi-Permanent

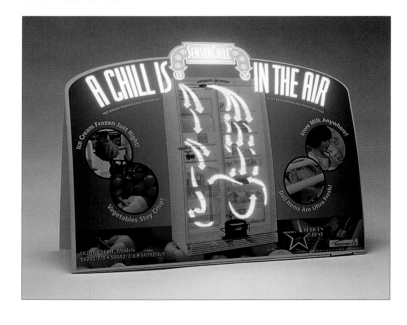

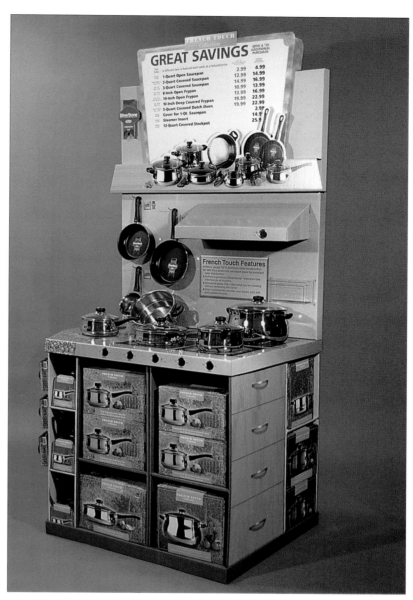

AWARD
Gold

TITLE
Ridgid Robo Hammer

CLIENT
Applied Concepts

ENTRANT
Midland Display Source
Franksville, WI

SUB-CATEGORY
Home and Industrial Tools
(including brooms, brushes, mops,
power saws, drills, drill bits, etc.)

DIVISION
Temporary

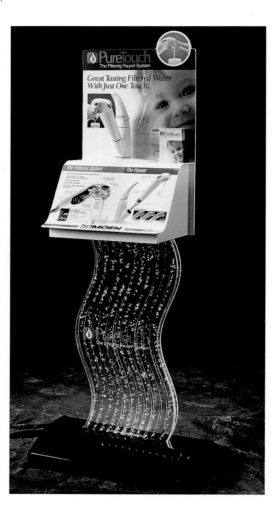

AWARD
Silver

TITLE
Pure Touch Bubbler

CLIENT
Moen Incorporated

ENTRANT
Downing Retail Display
Cleveland, OH

SUB-CATEGORY
Appliances
(large and small)

DIVISION
Permanent

AWARD
Silver

TITLE
Clopay Home Depot
Garage Door Showcase

CLIENT
Clopay Building Products Company

ENTRANT
Cannon Equipment
Rosemount, MN

SUB-CATEGORY
Building Supplies
(including paints and stains,
paneling, ceiling tiles, lighting and
fixtures, roofing materials, lumber,
siding, heating, plumbing, etc.)

DIVISION
Permanent

AWARD
Silver

TITLE
RoboLaser Counter Display

CLIENT
Toolz, Inc.

ENTRANT
Creative Solutions Group
Fairfield, NJ

SUB-CATEGORY
Home and Industrial Tools
(including brooms, brushes, mops,
power saws, drills, drill bits, etc.)

DIVISION
Permanent

AWARD
Silver

TITLE
Makita Power Tool Display

CLIENT
Makita USA, Inc.

ENTRANT
United Displaycraft
Des Plaines, IL

SUB-CATEGORY
Home and Industrial Tools
(including brooms, brushes, mops,
power saws, drills, drill bits, etc.)

DIVISION
Permanent

AWARD
Silver

TITLE
Leviton Modular Dimmer Display

CLIENT
Leviton Manufacturing Company

ENTRANT
Thomson-Leeds Company Inc.
Sunnyside, NY

SUB-CATEGORY
Home Furnishings and Housewares
(including household furniture, upholstery, carpeting,
wall and floor covering, fireplace accessories, patio and
lawn furnishings, linens, kitchen needs, towels, etc.)

DIVISION
Permanent

AWARD
Silver

TITLE
Braun Sam's Club Handblender Display

CLIENT
The Gillette Company

ENTRANT
Mechtronics Corporation
Stamford, CT

SUB-CATEGORY
Appliances
(large and small)

DIVISION
Semi-Permanent

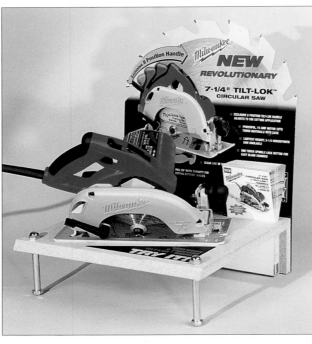

AWARD
Silver

TITLE
Tilt-Lok Circular Saw Wall/Counter Display

CLIENT
Milwaukee Electric Tool Corporation

ENTRANT
Innovative Marketing Solutions, Inc.
Bensenville, IL

SUB-CATEGORY
Home and Industrial Tools
(including brooms, brushes, mops,
power saws, drills, drill bits, etc.)

DIVISION
Semi-Permanent

AWARD
Silver

TITLE
Craftsman High-Wheel Weed
Trimmer Merchandise

CLIENT
Murray Inc.

ENTRANT
Bish Creative Display
Lake Zurich, IL

SUB-CATEGORY
Lawn and Garden Supplies
(including mowers, fertilizers, seeds,
spreaders, shovels, insecticides, pesticides, etc.)

DIVISION
Semi-Permanent

AWARD
Silver

TITLE
X-Treme Duck Tape 1/2 Side Kick

CLIENT
Manco, Inc.

ENTRANT
Packaging Corporation of America
Ashland, OH

SUB-CATEGORY
Home and Industrial Tools
(including brooms, brushes, mops,
power saws, drills, drill bits, etc.)

DIVISION
Temporary

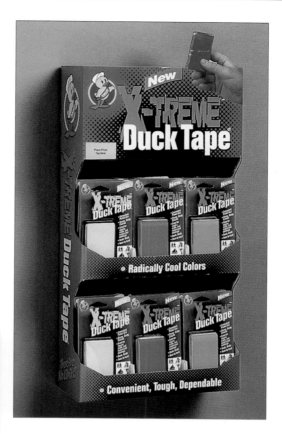

AWARD
Silver

TITLE
U.S. Flag Center Pallet Display

CLIENT
Valley Forge Flag Co., Inc.

ENTRANT
Triangle Display Group
Philadelphia, PA

SUB-CATEGORY
Home Furnishings and Housewares
(including household furniture, upholstery, carpeting,
wall and floor covering, fireplace accessories, patio and
lawn furnishings, linens, kitchen needs, towels, etc.)

DIVISION
Temporary

AWARD
Silver

TITLE
Simplicity Spring Pop Kit

CLIENT
Simplicity Manufacturing Inc.

ENTRANT
Bish Creative Display
Lake Zurich, IL

SUB-CATEGORY
Lawn and Garden Supplies
(including mowers, fertilizers, seeds,
spreaders, shovels, insecticides, pesticides, etc.)

DIVISION
Temporary

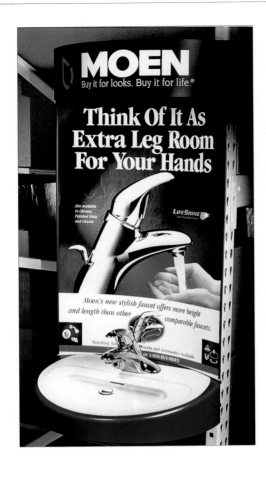

AWARD
Bronze

TITLE
Viletta Side Cap

CLIENT
Moen Incorporated

ENTRANT
Downing Retail Display
Cleveland, OH

SUB-CATEGORY
Appliances
(large and small)

DIVISION
Permanent

AWARD
Bronze

TITLE
Krylon Portable
Dolly Display

CLIENT
Krylon Products Group

ENTRANT
Downing Retail Display
Cleveland, OH

SUB-CATEGORY
Building Supplies
(including paints and stains, paneling, ceiling
tiles, lighting and fixtures, roofing materials,
lumber, siding, heating, plumbing, etc.)

DIVISION
Permanent

AWARD
Bronze

TITLE
Krylon Seasonal
Wire Display

CLIENT
Krylon Product Group

ENTRANT
Downing Retail Display
Cleveland, OH

SUB-CATEGORY
Building Supplies
(including paints and stains, paneling, ceiling
tiles, lighting and fixtures, roofing materials,
lumber, siding, heating, plumbing, etc.)

DIVISION
Permanent

AWARD
Bronze

TITLE
Illusions Display

CLIENT
Sherwin Williams

ENTRANT
**Instore Solutions
Dallas, TX**

SUB-CATEGORY
Building Supplies
(including paints and stains, paneling,
ceiling tiles, lighting and fixtures,
roofing materials, lumber, siding,
heating, plumbing, etc.)

DIVISION
Permanent

AWARD
Bronze

TITLE
RoboGrip II Demo Display

CLIENT
Applied Concepts, Inc.

ENTRANT
**Display Network, Inc.
West Chicago, IL**

SUB-CATEGORY
Home and Industrial Tools
(including brooms, brushes, mops,
power saws, drills, drill bits, etc.)

DIVISION
Permanent

AWARD
Bronze

TITLE
PowerMate Shelf Display

CLIENT
**Sunbeam Corportion (Canada)
Ltd.**

ENTRANT
**HMG Griffith Inc.
Toronto, ON, Canada**

SUB-CATEGORY
Home and Industrial Tools
(including brooms, brushes, mops,
power saws, drills, drill bits, etc.)

DIVISION
Permanent

AWARD
Bronze

TITLE
Congoleum Laminate Display

CLIENT
Congoleum Corporation

ENTRANT
AG Industries
Cleveland, OH

SUB-CATEGORY
Home Furnishings and Housewares
(including household furniture, upholstery, carpeting,
wall and floor covering, fireplace accessories, patio and
lawn furnishings, linens, kitchen needs, towels, etc.)

DIVISION
Permanent

Award
Bronze

TITLE
Raymond Waites Branded Rug Display

CLIENT
Beaulieu of America

ENTRANT
The Niven Marketing Group
Bensenville, IL

SUB-CATEGORY
Home Furnishings and Housewares
(including household furniture,
upholstery, carpeting, wall and
floor covering, fireplace accessories,
patio and lawn furnishings, linens,
kitchen needs, towels, etc.)

DIVISION
Permanent

AWARD
Bronze

TITLE
Hunter Douglas Soft Suede Demonstrator

CLIENT
Hunter Douglas Verticals Division

ENTRANT
Thomson-Leeds Company Inc.
Sunnyside, NY

SUB-CATEGORY
Home Furnishings and Housewares
(including household furniture, upholstery, carpeting,
wall and floor covering, fireplace accessories, patio and
lawn furnishings, linens, kitchen needs, towels, etc.)

DIVISION
Permanent

AWARD
Bronze

TITLE
"Expressions" Floor Sample Display

CLIENT
Perstorp Flooring

ENTRANT
ImageWorks Display & Marketing Group
Winston Salem, NC

SUB-CATEGORY
Home Furnishings and Housewares
(including household furniture, upholstery, carpeting,
wall and floor covering, fireplace accessories, patio
and lawn furnishings, linens, kitchen needs, towels, etc.)

DIVISION
Semi-Permanent

AWARD
Bronze

TITLE
Crackling Hearth Logg Display

CLIENT
Clorox Company

ENTRANT
Rapid Displays
Union City, CA,

SUB-CATEGORY
Home Furnishings
and Housewares
(including household furniture,
upholstery, carpeting, wall and floor
covering, fireplace accessories, patio
and lawn furnishings, linens, kitchen
needs, towels, etc.)

DIVISION
Semi-Permanent

AWARD
Bronze

TITLE
Candle Corp. Pallet Display

CLIENT
Candle Corporation of America

ENTRANT
Smurfit-Stone Display Group
Richmond, VA

SUB-CATEGORY
Home Furnishings
and Housewares
(including household furniture,
upholstery, carpeting, wall and floor
covering, fireplace accessories, patio
and lawn furnishings, linens, kitchen
needs, towels, etc.)

DIVISION
Semi-Permanent

Award
Bronze

TITLE
340 Series Stream Rotor Display

CLIENT
The Toro Company, Irrigation Division

ENTRANT
JP Marketing Services
Santa Fe Springs, CA

SUB-CATEGORY
Lawn and Garden Supplies
(including mowers, fertilizers, seeds, spreaders,
shovels, insecticides, pesticides, etc.)

DIVISION
Semi-Permanent

AWARD
Bronze

TITLE
Minami Icicle Demonstrator

CLIENT
Minami Intl

ENTRANT
Thomson-Leeds Company Inc.
Sunnyside, NY

SUB-CATEGORY
Building Supplies
(including paints and stains, paneling, ceiling tiles,
lighting and fixtures, roofing materials, lumber,
siding, heating, plumbing, etc.)

DIVISION
Temporary

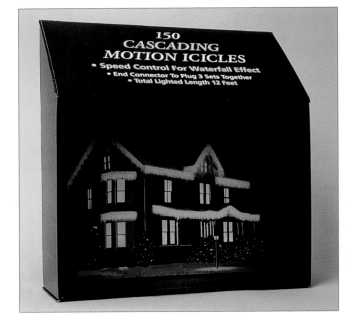

AWARD
Bronze

TITLE
Ridge Tool Tubing Cutter Display

CLIENT
Ridge Tool Company

ENTRANT
Packaging Corporation of America
Ashland, OH

SUB-CATEGORY
Home and Industrial Tools
(including brooms, brushes, mops,
power saws, drills, drill bits, etc.)

DIVISION
Temporary

AWARD
Gold/Display-of-the-Year

TITLE
Everland Kid City Interactive Kiosk

CLIENT
Word Entertainment

ENTRANT
Trans World Marketing
East Rutherford, NJ

SUB-CATEGORY
Interactive

DIVISION
Permanent

AWARD
Silver

TITLE
Burger King Virtual Fun Center

CLIENT
Burger King Corporation

ENTRANT
Frank Mayer & Associates, Inc.
Grafton, WI

SUB-CATEGORY
Interactive

DIVISION
Permanent

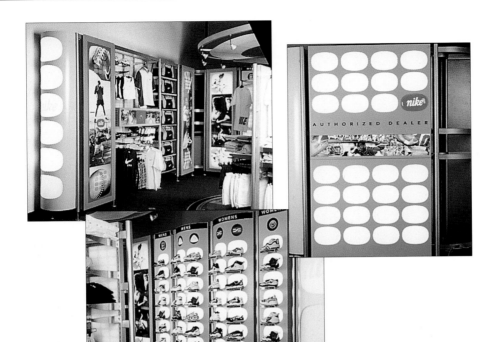

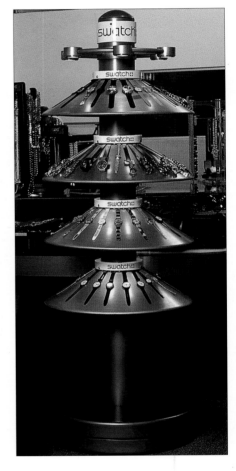

AWARD
Gold

TITLE
Nike "Kit O Parts"

CLIENT
Nike Inc.

ENTRANT
RTC Industries, Inc.
Rolling Meadows, IL

SUB-CATEGORY
Footwear and Shoe Care

DIVISION
Permanent

AWARD
Gold

TITLE
Swatch Cone Tower

CLIENT
Mr. Jim Kenny (Swatch USA)

ENTRANT
Darko Company Inc.
Twinsburg, OH

SUB-CATEGORY
Jewelry
(including billfolds, eyewear,
fine pens and pencils, luggage,
sunglasses, fine lighters, etc.)

DIVISION
Permanent

AWARD
Gold

TITLE
Skechers 3D Giant Slatwall Logo Block

CLIENT
Skechers USA

ENTRANT
Skechers USA
Manhattan Beach, CA

SUB-CATEGORY
Footwear and Shoe Care

DIVISION
Semi-Permanent

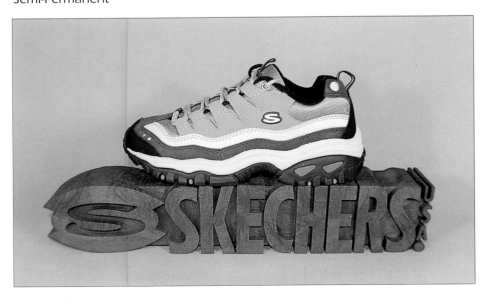

AWARD
Silver

TITLE
Nike Satellite

CLIENT
Nike Inc.

ENTRANT
RTC Industries, Inc.
Rolling Meadows, IL

SUB-CATEGORY
Apparel and Sewing Notions

DIVISION
Permanent

AWARD
Silver

TITLE
Skechers USA 12 Shoe
Pedestal Display

CLIENT
Skechers USA

ENTRANT
United Displaycraft
Des Plaines, IL

SUB-CATEGORY
Footwear and Shoe Care

DIVISION
Permanent

AWARD
Silver

TITLE
Airlift Backpack Display

CLIENT
Jansport

ENTRANT
Frank Mayer & Associates, Inc.
Grafton, WI

SUB-CATEGORY
Jewelry
(including billfolds, eyewear,
fine pens and pencils, luggage,
sunglasses, fine lighters, etc.)

DIVISION
Permanent

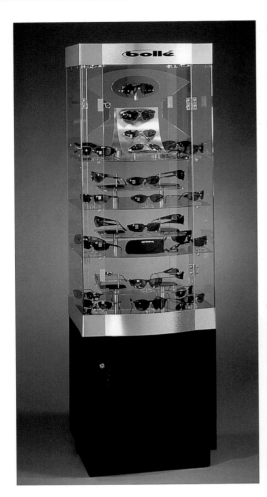

AWARD
Silver

TITLE
Bollé Display Tower

CLIENT
Bollé

ENTRANT
New Dimensions Research Corporation
Melville, NY

SUB-CATEGORY
Jewelry
(including billfolds, eyewear, fine pens and
pencils, luggage, sunglasses, fine lighters, etc.)

DIVISION
Permanent

AWARD
Silver

TITLE
AT&T Wireless
PrePaid Counter Display

CLIENT
AT&T

ENTRANT
Design Phase, Inc.
Northbrook, IL

SUB-CATEGORY
Telecommunications
(telephones, fax machines, etc.)

DIVISION
Permanent

AWARD
Silver

TITLE
Motorola, Inc.
AAD Showroom P.O.P. Kit

CLIENT
Motorola, Inc. -
Accessories & Aftermarket

ENTRANT
DCI Marketing
Milwaukee, WI

SUB-CATEGORY
Personal Telecommunications
(cellular phones, pagers, etc.)

DIVISION
Permanent

AWARD
Silver

TITLE
Kmart Girls Lee Rider Pallet Display

CLIENT
VF Jeanswear, Inc.

ENTRANT
ImageWorks Display & Marketing Group
Winston Salem, NC

SUB-CATEGORY
Apparel and Sewing Notions

DIVISION
Semi-Permanent

AWARD
Silver

TITLE
Transitions Sunlense
Counter Unit

CLIENT
St. George Group

ENTRANT
C.D. Baird & Co., Inc.
West Allis, WI

SUB-CATEGORY
Jewelry
(including billfolds, eyewear,
fine pens and pencils, luggage,
sunglasses, fine lighters, etc.)

DIVISION
Semi-Permanent

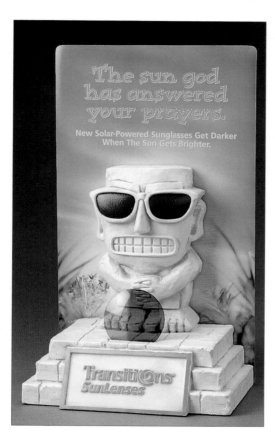

AWARD
Silver

TITLE
NikeTown Snowflakes

CLIENT
Nike, Inc.

ENTRANT
Rapid Displays
Union City, CA

SUB-CATEGORY
Apparel and Sewing Notions

DIVISION
Temporary

AWARD
Silver

TITLE
Dr. Scholl's Magna Energy
12pc. FS/PW

CLIENT
Schering Plough Health Care
Products

ENTRANT
Advertising Display Company
Lyndhurst, NJ

SUB-CATEGORY
Footwear and Shoe Care

DIVISION
Temporary

AWARD
Silver

TITLE
Sprint Phone Dangler

CLIENT
DraftWorldwide for Sprint

ENTRANT
Rapid Displays
Chicago, IL

SUB-CATEGORY
Telecommunications
(telephones, fax machines, etc.)

DIVISION
Temporary

AWARD
Bronze

TITLE
Inneractive Floor Fixture

CLIENT
Nike Inc.

ENTRANT
JP Marketing Services
Santa Fe Springs, CA

SUB-CATEGORY
Apparel and Sewing Notions

DIVISION
Permanent

AWARD
Bronze

TITLE
Gravis Shoe Tower

CLIENT
Gravis

ENTRANT
JP Marketing Services
Santa Fe Springs, CA

SUB-CATEGORY
Footwear and Shoe Care

DIVISION
Permanent

AWARD
Bronze

TITLE
No Nonsense Renew!
Sawtooth Display

CLIENT
Kayser-Roth Corporation

ENTRANT
New Dimensions
Research Corporation
Melville, NY

SUB-CATEGORY
Apparel and Sewing Notions

DIVISION
Permanent

AWARD
Bronze

TITLE
Skechers USA 24 Shoe
Racetrack Floor Display

CLIENT
Skechers USA

ENTRANT
United Displaycraft
Des Plaines, IL

SUB-CATEGORY
Footwear and Shoe Care

DIVISION
Permanent

AWARD
Bronze

TITLE
Skechers USA 5 Shelf Wall Display

CLIENT
Skechers USA

ENTRANT
United Displaycraft
Des Plaines, IL

SUB-CATEGORY
Footwear and Shoe Care

DIVISION
Permanent

AWARD
Bronze

TITLE
Monet Hoop Display

CLIENT
The Monet Group

ENTRANT
Trans World Marketing
East Rutherford, NJ

SUB-CATEGORY
Jewelry
(including billfolds, eyewear,
fine pens and pencils, luggage,
sunglasses, fine lighters, etc.)

DIVISION
Permanent

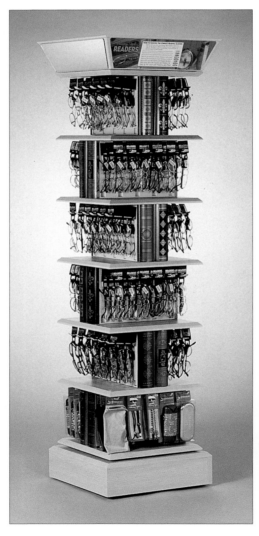

AWARD
Bronze

TITLE
Panama Jack Reader Floor Display

CLIENT
Panama Jack Environmental
Optics

ENTRANT
Henschel-Steinau, Inc.
Englewood, NJ

SUB-CATEGORY
Jewelry
(including billfolds, eyewear,
fine pens and pencils, luggage,
sunglasses, fine lighters, etc.)

DIVISION
Permanent

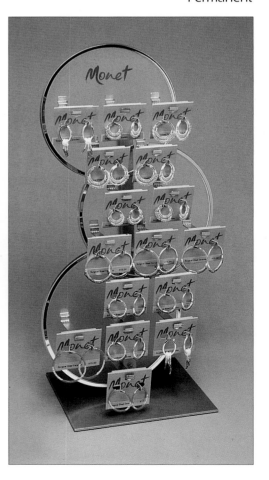

AWARD
Bronze

TITLE
Nine West Eyewear Displays

CLIENT
Safilo Group

ENTRANT
Trans World Marketing
East Rutherford, NJ

SUB-CATEGORY
Jewelry
(including billfolds, eyewear,
fine pens and pencils, luggage,
sunglasses, fine lighters, etc.)

DIVISION
Permanent

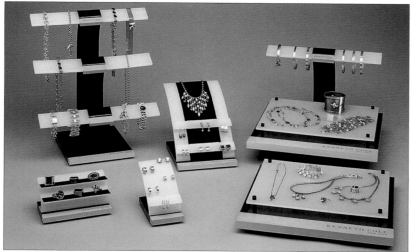

AWARD
Bronze

TITLE
Kenneth Cole Case Presentation

CLIENT
Swank, Inc.

ENTRANT
Trans World Marketing
East Rutherford, NJ

SUB-CATEGORY
Jewelry
(including billfolds, eyewear,
fine pens and pencils, luggage,
sunglasses, fine lighters, etc.)

DIVISION
Permanent

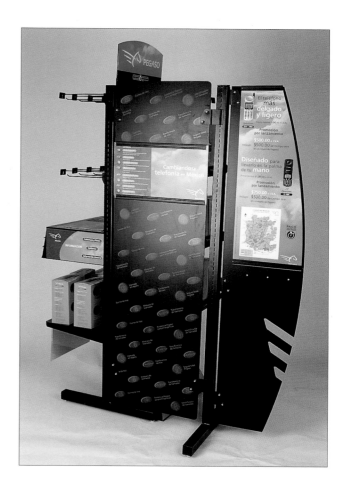

AWARD
Bronze

TITLE
Pegaso Phone in a Box

CLIENT
Pegaso PCS, SA de CV

ENTRANT
RPA
Mexico, D.F., Mexico

SUB-CATEGORY
Personal Telecommunications
(cellular phones, pagers, etc.)

DIVISION
Permanent

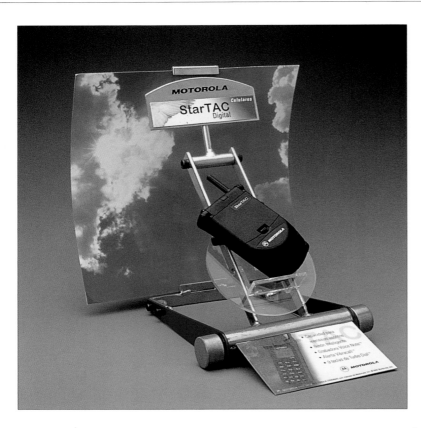

AWARD
Bronze

TITLE
Motorola Cell Phone Display

CLIENT
Motorola

ENTRANT
RPA
Mexico, D.F., Mexico

SUB-CATEGORY
Personal Telecommunications
(cellular phones, pagers, etc.)

DIVISION
Permanent

AWARD
Bronze

TITLE
iPhone Counter Display

CLIENT
Infogear Technology Corp.

RAPID DISPLAYS
Union City, CA

SUB-CATEGORY
Telecommunications
(telephones, fax machines, etc.)

DIVISION
Permanent

AWARD
Bronze

TITLE
Qualcomm Thin Phone Display

CLIENT
Qualcomm

ENTRANT
JP Marketing Services
Santa Cruz, CA

SUB-CATEGORY
Telecommunications
(telephones, fax machines, etc.)

DIVISION
Permanent

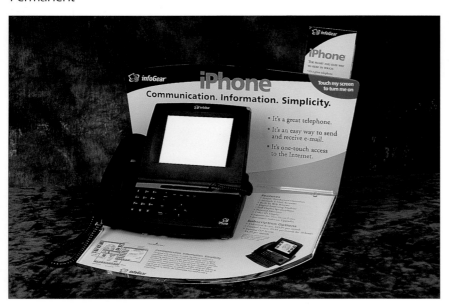

AWARD
Bronze

TITLE
Skechers Kids Acrylic Logo Block

CLIENT
Skechers USA

ENTRANT
Skechers USA
Manhattan Beach, CA

SUB-CATEGORY
Footwear and Shoe Care

DIVISION
Semi-Permanent

AWARD
Bronze

TITLE
Skechers Collection Acrylic
Logo Block

CLIENT
Skechers USA

ENTRANT
Skechers USA
Manhattan Beach, CA

SUB-CATEGORY
Footwear and Shoe Care

DIVISION
Semi-Permanent

AWARD
Bronze

TITLE
Estée Lauder Charm
Merchandiser

CLIENT
Estée Lauder Inc.

ENTRANT
IDMD Manufacturing Inc.
Toronto, ON, Canada

SUB-CATEGORY
Jewelry
(including billfolds, eyewear,
fine pens and pencils, luggage,
sunglasses, fine lighters, etc.)

DIVISION
Semi-Permanent

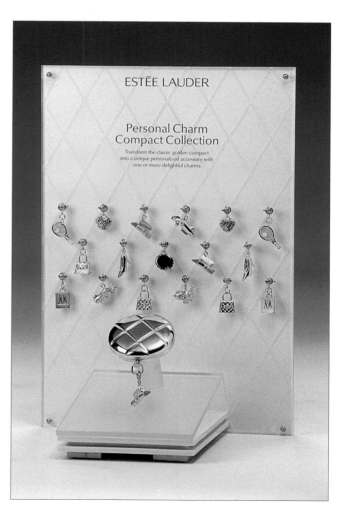

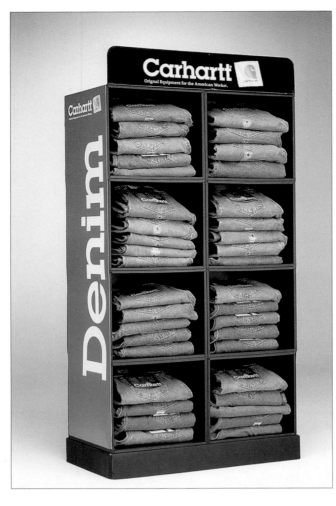

AWARD
Bronze

TITLE
Carhartt Denim Pallet Display

CLIENT
Carhartt

ENTRANT
Meridian Display & Merchandising
Saint Paul, MN

SUB-CATEGORY
Apparel and Sewing Notions

DIVISION
Temporary

AWARD
Bronze

TITLE
Nike Footaction
6453 Floor Display

CLIENT
Nike, Inc.

ENTRANT
Rapid Displays
Union City, CA

SUB-CATEGORY
Footwear and Shoe Care

DIVISION
Temporary

AWARD
Bronze

TITLE
Sprint Holiday Tree

CLIENT
Sprint

ENTRANT
Rapid Displays
Chicago, IL

SUB-CATEGORY
Telecommunications
(telephones, fax machines, etc.)

DIVISION
Temporary

AWARD
Gold

TITLE
Imperial Alexander Julian Display

CLIENT
Imperial Home Décor Group

ENTRANT
AG Industries
Cleveland, OH

SUB-CATEGORY
Other

DIVISION
Permanent

AWARD
Silver

TITLE
Rexall Sundown Shelf System
& Powerwing

CLIENT
Rexall Sundown

ENTRANT
Phoenix Display/
International Paper
Thorofare, NJ

SUB-CATEGORY
Other

DIVISION
Permanent

AWARD
Silver

TITLE
GNC Vitamin Family
Glorifier

CLIENT
General Nutrition Corp.

ENTRANT
Henschel-Steinau, Inc.
Englewood, NJ

SUB-CATEGORY
Other

DIVISION
Semi-Permanent

AWARD
Silver

TITLE
FrigoPub Nestle Buitoni
Italian Meal Centre

CLIENT
Nestle U.S.A.

ENTRANT
Octagon Industries Inc.
Toronto, ON, Canada

SUB-CATEGORY
Supermarkets

DIVISION
Temporary

AWARD
Bronze

TITLE
Destination Star Wars Program

CLIENT
Hasbro, Inc. (with Lucas Licensing LTD)

ENTRANT
RTC Industries, Inc.
Rolling Meadows, IL

SUB-CATEGORY
Other

DIVISION
Permanent

AWARD
Bronze

TITLE
Staples Y2K Kiosk

CLIENT
Staples

ENTRANT
Inland Consumer
Packaging and Displays
Indianapolis, IN

SUB-CATEGORY
Other

DIVISION
Temporary

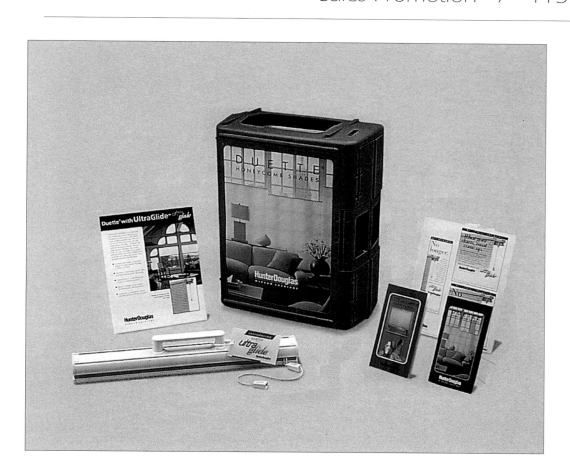

AWARD
Gold

TITLE
Manhattan/Duette Sample Case

CLIENT
Hunter Douglas

ENTRANT
Thomson-Leeds Company Inc.
Sunnyside, NY

SUB-CATEGORY
National - entries used in the
majority of the country of origin

DIVISION
Permanent

AWARD
Gold

TITLE
Microsoft Office 2000

CLIENT
Microsoft

ENTRANT
Ivy Hill/Warner Media Services
Glendale, CA

SUB-CATEGORY
National - entries used in the
majority of the country of origin

DIVISION
Temporary

Standee

Counter Card

Press Kit

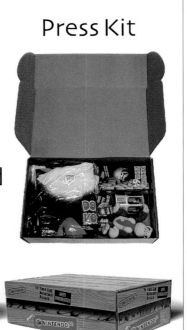

AWARD
Gold/Display-of-the-Year

TITLE
Donkey Kong 64 Sales Promotion

CLIENT
Nintendo of America

ENTRANT
The Corporate Image
Seattle, WA

SUB-CATEGORY
National - entries used in the
majority of the country of origin

DIVISION
Semi-Permanent

AWARD
Silver

TITLE
Sears Blue's Clues Treasure Hunt

CLIENT
Schwarz Worlwide Sears

ENTRANT
Rapid Displays
Chicago, IL

SUB-CATEGORY
National - entries used in the
majority of the country of origin

DIVISION
Temporary

AWARD
Silver

TITLE
Denny's/Wishbone Holiday Promotion

CLIENT
Denny's

ENTRANT
TIC TOC and U.S. Display
Dallas, TX

SUB-CATEGORY
National - entries used in the
majority of the country of origin

DIVISION
Temporary

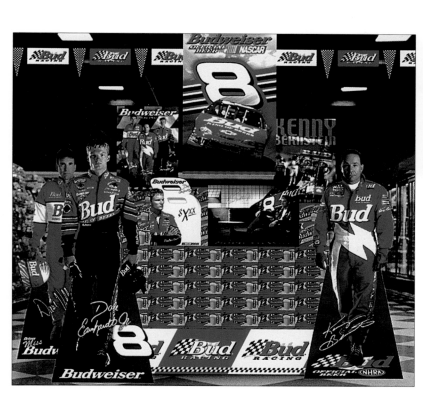

AWARD
Bronze

TITLE
Bud Racing Program

CLIENT
Anheuser-Busch, Inc.

ENTRANT
Anheuser-Busch, Inc.
Saint Louis, MO

SUB-CATEGORY
National - entries used in
the majority of the country
of origin

DIVISION
Semi-Permanent

AWARD
Bronze

TITLE
Bud Bowl Program

CLIENT
Anheuser-Busch, Inc.

ENTRANT
Anheuser-Busch, Inc.
Saint Louis, MO

SUB-CATEGORY
National - entries used in
the majority of the country
of origin

DIVISION
Temporary

AWARD
Bronze

TITLE
Walt Disney/Pixar Toy Story II

CLIENT
The Walt Disney Co.-
Consumer Products

ENTRANT
Creative Solutions Group
Fairfield, NJ

SUB-CATEGORY
National - entries used in the
majority of the country of origin

DIVISION
Temporary

AWARD
Bronze

TITLE
Aussie Promotional Floor
Dsiplay

CLIENT
Bristol Myers Squibb Canada

ENTRANT
Point 1 Displays Inc.
Montreal, Quebec, Canada

SUB-CATEGORY
National - entries used
in the majority of
the country of origin

DIVISION
Temporary

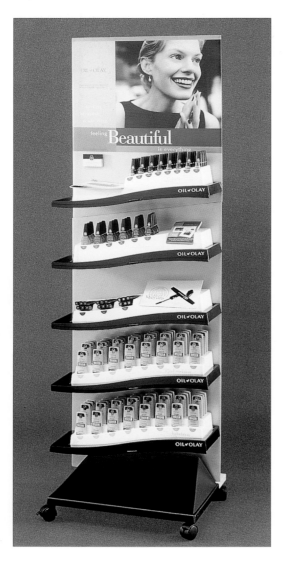

AWARD
Bronze

TITLE
Olay Cosmetics "I Am Beautiful"
Program

CLIENT
Procter & Gamble

ENTRANT
Rock-Tenn Company/Alliance Group
Winston Salem, NC

SUB-CATEGORY
National - entries used in the
majority of the country of origin

DIVISION
Temporary

AWARD
Gold

TITLE
Stouffer's Soup Station Merchandiser

CLIENT
Nestle Foodservices

ENTRANT
HMG Griffith Inc.
Toronto, ON, Canada

SUB-CATEGORY
Quick Service Food Restaurants

DIVISION
Permanent

AWARD
Gold

TITLE
McDonald's Disney Millennium Kiosk

CLIENT
Schwarz Worldwide for McDonald's
Corporation

ENTRANT
Rapid Displays
Chicago, IL

SUB-CATEGORY
Quick Service Food Restaurants

DIVISION
Temporary

AWARD
Gold

TITLE
Taco Bell-Talking Chihuahuas
Counter Unit

CLIENT
Wunderman Cato Johnson

ENTRANT
Rapid Displays
Chicago, IL

SUB-CATEGORY
Quick Service Food Restaurants

DIVISION
Temporary

AWARD
Silver

TITLE
Fed Ex ComLink

CLIENT
Fed Ex

ENTRANT
Advertising Display Company
Lyndhurst, NJ

SUB-CATEGORY
Professional Services
(including banks, travel agencies,
real estate, telecommunications, air,
sea and land transportation, etc.)

DIVISION
Permanent

AWARD
Silver

TITLE
California State Lottery Playcenter

CLIENT
California State Lottery

ENTRANT
Alcone Marketing Group
Irvine, CA

SUB-CATEGORY
Other Services and Establishments
(including trade, craft and
mobile advertising, etc.)

DIVISION
Permanent

AWARD
Silver

TITLE
Dairy Queen Orange Julius

CLIENT
International Dairy Queen

ENTRANT
DCI Marketing
Milwaukee, WI

SUB-CATEGORY
Quick Service Food Restaurants

DIVISION
Permanent

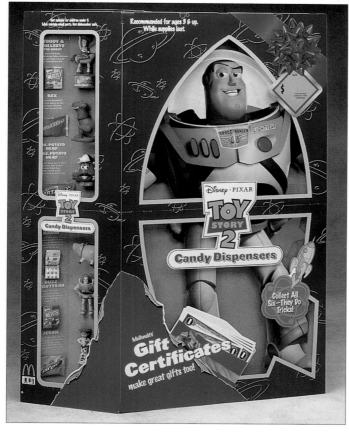

AWARD
Silver

TITLE
McDonald's Toy Story 2 Kiosk

CLIENT
Schwarz Worldwide for
McDonald's Corporation

ENTRANT
Rapid Displays
Chicago, IL

SUB-CATEGORY
Quick Service Food Restaurants

DIVISION
Temporary

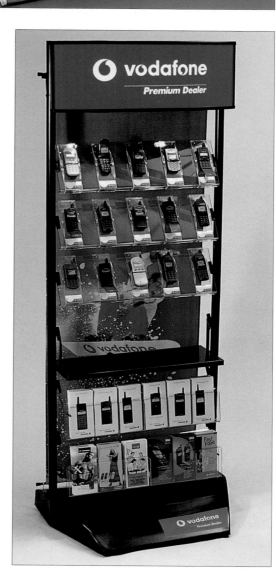

AWARD
Bronze

TITLE
Mobile Phone Instore Display

CLIENT
Vodafone Pty Ltd

ENTRANT
Efficiency Displays (Marketing) Pty
Ltd
Brookvale, Australia

SUB-CATEGORY
Professional Services
(including banks, travel agencies, real
estate, telecommunications, air, sea and
land transportation, etc.)

DIVISION
Permanent

AWARD
Bronze

TITLE
Netcom Info Cener

CLIENT
Netcom GSM ASA

ENTRANT
Leo Burnett Oslo
Oslo, Norway

SUB-CATEGORY
Professional Services
(including banks, travel agencies,
 real estate, telecommunications,
 air, sea and land transportation, etc.)

DIVISION
Permanent

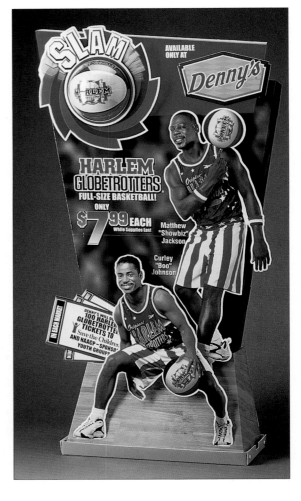

AWARD
Bronze

TITLE
Denny's Harlem
Globetrotters Standee

CLIENT
Alcone Marketing Group

ENTRANT
C.D. Baird & Co., Inc.
West Allis, WI

SUB-CATEGORY
Quick Service Food
Restaurants

DIVISION
Temporary

AWARD
Bronze

TITLE
Taco Bell Chihuahuas Motion Display

CLIENT
Wunderman Cato Johnson

ENTRANT
Rapid Displays
Chicago, IL

SUB-CATEGORY
Quick Service Food Restaurants

DIVISION
Temporary

AWARD
Gold

TITLE
Norwegian Sky Mobile

CLIENT
Alison Group

ENTRANT
Promo Edge Division of Menasha
Corporation
Menomonee Falls, WI

SUB-CATEGORY
Signage Category

DIVISION
Temporary

AWARD
Silver

TITLE
Miller Lite Double-Sided Hanging Neon

CLIENT
Miller Brewing Company

ENTRANT
Fallon Luminous Products
Spartanburg, SC

SUB-CATEGORY
Signage Category

DIVISION
Permanent

AWARD
Silver

TITLE
Bud Racing Dimensional Banner

CLIENT
Anheuser-Busch, Inc.

ENTRANT
Anheuser-Busch, Inc.
Saint Louis, MO

SUB-CATEGORY
Signage Category

DIVISION
Semi-Permanent

AWARD
Bronze

TITLE
Take Your Best Shot - Sign Animator

CLIENT
United Distillers & Vintners

ENTRANT
Creative Solutions Group
Fairfield, NJ

SUB-CATEGORY
Signage Category

DIVISION
Permanent

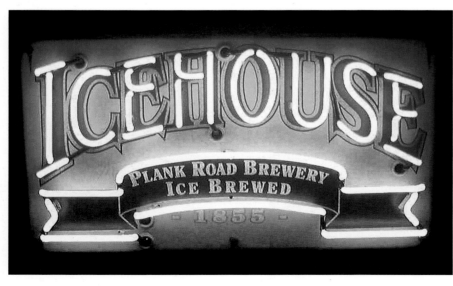

AWARD
Bronze

TITLE
Icehouse Classic Neon

CLIENT
Miller Brewing Company
Fallon Luminous Products

ENTRANT
Spartanburg, SC

SUB-CATEGORY
Signage Category

DIVISION
Permanent

AWARD
Bronze

TITLE
Camel Motion Sign

CLIENT
R.J. Reynolds, Intenational

ENTRANT
Heritage Sign & Display
Nesquehoning, PA

SUB-CATEGORY
Signage Category

DIVISION
Permanent

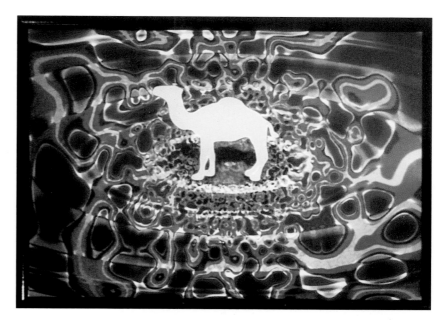

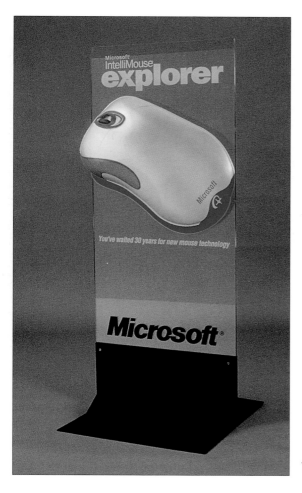

AWARD
Bronze

TITLE
IntelliMouse Explorer Marquee

CLIENT
Microsoft

ENTRANT
Promo Edge
Division of Menasha Corporation
Menomonee Falls, WI

SUB-CATEGORY
Signage Category

DIVISION
Semi-Permanent

AWARD
Bronze

TITLE
Hunter Douglas Duette
Ultra Glide Sign

CLIENT
Hunter Douglas

ENTRANT
Thomson-Leeds Company Inc.
Sunnyside, NY

SUB-CATEGORY
Signage Category

DIVISION
Semi-Permanent

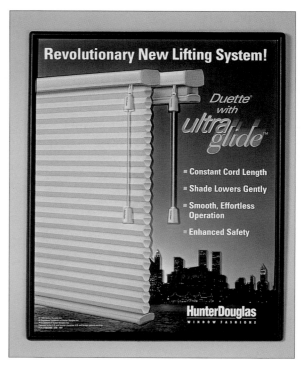

AWARD
Gold

TITLE
Pringles Center Stage

CLIENT
Procter & Gamble Co.

ENTRANT
Rand Display, Inc.
Teaneck, NJ

SUB-CATEGORY
Snacks, Cookies and Crackers

DIVISION
Permanent

AWARD
Gold

TITLE
Lance Cape Cod Lighthouse
End Cap

CLIENT
Lance, Inc.

ENTRANT
Stainless Metal Products, Inc.
Chattanooga, TN

SUB-CATEGORY
Snacks, Cookies and Crackers

DIVISION
Permanent

AWARD
Gold

TITLE
Barnum's Marine Tower

CLIENT
Nabisco Biscuit Co.

ENTRANT
Creative Solutions Group
Fairfield, NJ

SUB-CATEGORY
Snacks, Cookies and Crackers

DIVISION
Semi-Permanent

AWARD
Gold

TITLE
Pepsi/Star Wars Life-Size
Character Display

CLIENT
Pepsi-Cola

ENTRANT
TIC TOC -
"The Imagination Company!"
Dallas, TX

SUB-CATEGORY
Soft Drinks, Mineral Waters
and Powdered Mixes

DIVISION
Semi-Permanent

AWARD
Gold

TITLE
Nabisco/Sony Cool School
Bus Display

CLIENT
Nabisco

ENTRANT
Oxford Innovations,
Division of Tim-Bar Corp.
New Oxford, PA

SUB-CATEGORY
Snacks, Cookies and Crackers

DIVISION
Temporary

AWARD
Silver

TITLE
Wrigley Eclipse Merchandiser
(V & H)

CLIENT
William Wrigley

ENTRANT
Advertising Display Company
Lyndhurst, NJ

SUB-CATEGORY
Candy, Gum and Mints

DIVISION
Permanent

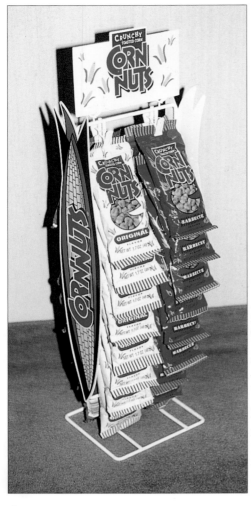

AWARD
Silver

TITLE
Nabisco Corn Nuts Counter Display

CLIENT
Nabisco

ENTRANT
United Displaycraft
Des Plaines, IL

SUB-CATEGORY
Snacks, Cookies and Crackers

DIVISION
Permanent

AWARD
Silver

TITLE
Coca-Cola Icon Bottle Merchandiser

CLIENT
Coca-Cola Company

ENTRANT
Paul Flum Ideas, Inc.
Saint Louis, MO

SUB-CATEGORY
Soft Drinks, Mineral Waters and
Powdered Mixes

DIVISION
Permanent

AWARD
Silver

TITLE
Coca-Cola Powerglide

CLIENT
The Coca-Cola Company Bottlers

ENTRANT
RTC Industries, Inc.
Rolling Meadows, IL

SUB-CATEGORY
Soft Drinks, Mineral Waters and
Powdered Mixes

DIVISION
Permanent

AWARD
Silver

TITLE
Cool Blasts Counter Display

CLIENT
Nabisco Foods Company

ENTRANT
ImageWorks Display &
Marketing Group
Winston Salem, NC

SUB-CATEGORY
Candy, Gum and Mints

DIVISION
Semi-Permanent

AWARD
Silver

TITLE
Cool Fruits-Fruit Power Prod.
Intro.

CLIENT
Cool Fruits Inc.

ENTRANT
Taurus Packaging
Cherry Hill, NJ

SUB-CATEGORY
Snacks, Cookies and Crackers

DIVISION
Semi-Permanent

AWARD
Bronze

TITLE
Albertson's End Cap Rack

CLIENT
Nabisco Biscuit Co.

ENTRANT
Creative Solutions Group
Fairfield, NJ

SUB-CATEGORY
Snacks, Cookies and Crackers

DIVISION
Permanent

AWARD
Bronze

TITLE
Lays Adjustable Route
Trade Display

CLIENT
The Smiths Snackfood
Company Ltd

ENTRANT
Efficiency Displays
(Marketing) Pty Ltd
Brookvale, Australia

SUB-CATEGORY
Snacks, Cookies and Crackers

DIVISION
Permanent

AWARD
Bronze

TITLE
Mountain Dew Bottle Neon

CLIENT
Pepsi-Cola Company

ENTRANT
Everbrite, Inc.
Greenfield, WI

SUB-CATEGORY
Soft Drinks, Mineral Waters
and Powdered Mixes

DIVISION
Permanent

AWARD
Bronze

TITLE
Coca-Cola Petroleum Forecourt Trolley

CLIENT
Coca-Cola South Pacific

ENTRANT
EGR Display & Coca-Cola South Pacific
Sydney, Darra, Australia

SUB-CATEGORY
Soft Drinks, Mineral Waters and
Powdered Mixes

DIVISION
Permanent

AWARD
Bronze

TITLE
Coca-Cola Retro Gas Pump 10

CLIENT
Coca-Cola

ENTRANT
HMG Worldwide
New York, NY

SUB-CATEGORY
Soft Drinks, Mineral Waters and
Powdered Mixes

DIVISION
Permanent

AWARD
Bronze

TITLE
Whipper Snapple Blender
Floorstand

CLIENT
Triarc Beverage Group, Inc.

ENTRANT
Mechtronics Corporation
Stamford, CT

SUB-CATEGORY
Soft Drinks, Mineral Waters
and Powdered Mixes

DIVISION
Permanent

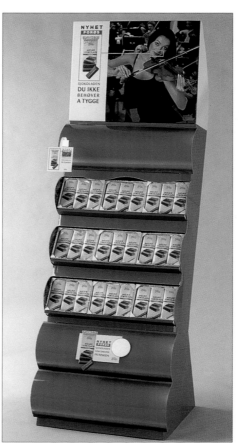

AWARD
Bronze

TITLE
Kraft Friea 'Porous Chocolate'
Display

CLIENT
Kraft Jacob Suchard - Freia AS

ENTRANT
Leo Burnett Oslo
Oslo, Norway

SUB-CATEGORY
Candy, Gum and Mints

DIVISION
Semi-Permanent

AWARD
Bronze

TITLE
Arnott's Deli Cracker Unit

CLIENT
Arnott's Biscuits Limited

ENTRANT
Arnott's Biscuits Limited
Sydney, Australia

SUB-CATEGORY
Snacks, Cookies and Crackers

DIVISION
Semi-Permanent

AWARD
Bronze

TITLE
Holiday Brick Cookie House

CLIENT
Archway-Mother's Cookie Company

ENTRANT
Chesapeake Display & Packaging
Winston Salem, NC

SUB-CATEGORY
Snacks, Cookies and Crackers

DIVISION
Semi-Permanent

AWARD
Bronze

TITLE
Wal-Mart Beverage Retail Ready Pallet Display

CLIENT
Kraft Foods, Inc.

ENTRANT
Great Northern Corporation
Racine, WI

SUB-CATEGORY
Soft Drinks, Mineral Waters and Powdered Mixes

DIVISION
Semi-Permanent

AWARD
Bronze

TITLE
Lollipop Paint Shop Ladder Display

CLIENT
Impact Confections

ENTRANT
Oxford Innovations,
Division of Tim-Bar Corp.
New Oxford, PA

SUB-CATEGORY
Candy, Gum and Mints

DIVISION
Temporary

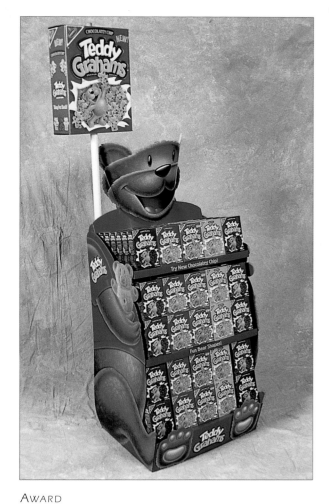

AWARD
Bronze

TITLE
Teddy Grahams Floorstand

CLIENT
Nabisco Biscuit Co.

ENTRANT
Creative Solutions Group
Fairfield, NJ

SUB-CATEGORY
Snacks, Cookies and Crackers

DIVISION
Temporary

AWARD
Bronze

TITLE
Nabisco March Madness
Lobby Display

CLIENT
Nabisco

ENTRANT
Oxford Innovations,
Division of Tim-Bar Corp.
New Oxford, PA

SUB-CATEGORY
Snacks, Cookies and Crackers

DIVISION
Temporary

AWARD
Bronze

TITLE
Nabisco Super Bowl Lobby Display

CLIENT
Nabisco

ENTRANT
Oxford Innovations,
Division of Tim-Bar Corp.
New Oxford, PA

SUB-CATEGORY
Snacks, Cookies and Crackers

DIVISION
Temporary

AWARD
Bronze

TITLE
Keeble Soup Can Disply

CLIENT
Keebler Company

ENTRANT
Smurfit-Stone Display Group
Richmond, VA

SUB-CATEGORY
Snacks, Cookies and Crackers

DIVISION
Temporary

AWARD
Bronze

TITLE
A & W Halloween
Munster Display

CLIENT
Dr. Pepper/7UP Inc.

ENTRANT
Bish Creative Display
Lake Zurich, IL

SUB-CATEGORY
Soft Drinks, Mineral Waters
and Powdered Mixes

DIVISION
Temporary

AWARD
Bronze

TITLE
7UP Scoreboard Display

CLIENT
Dr. Pepper/7UP Inc.

ENTRANT
Bish Creative Display
Lake Zurich, IL

SUB-CATEGORY
Soft Drinks, Mineral Waters
and Powdered Mixes

DIVISION
Temporary

AWARD
Gold

TITLE
EV Global Dealership Display

CLIENT
EV Global Motors, Inc.

ENTRANT
Frank Mayer & Associates, Inc.
Grafton, WI

SUB-CATEGORY
Sports Equipment
(including bicycles, etc.)

DIVISION
Permanent

AWARD
Gold

TITLE
Dunlop-Maxfli Glove Display
& Fitting Device

CLIENT
Dunlop-Maxfli

ENTRANT
DCI Marketing
Milwaukee, WI

SUB-CATEGORY
Sports Equipment
(including bicycles, etc.)

DIVISION
Permanent

AWARD
Gold

TITLE
Century of Bears

CLIENT
RNR Inc.

ENTRANT
Kell Specialty Products
Chippewa Falls, WI

SUB-CATEGORY
Toys

DIVISION
Semi-Permanent

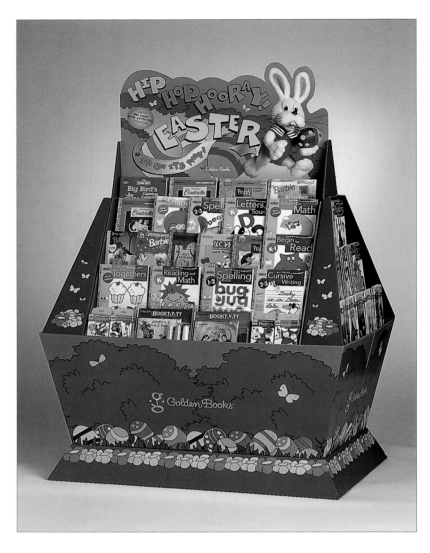

AWARD
Gold

TITLE
Golden Books Easter Basket

CLIENT
Golden Books Publishing

ENTRANT
Smurfit-Stone Display Group
Richmond, VA

SUB-CATEGORY
Books, Newspapers and Magazines

DIVISION
Temporary

AWARD
Gold

TITLE
D.K./NFL Interactive Merchandiser

CLIENT
D.K. Publishing

ENTRANT
Taurus Packaging
Cherry Hill, NJ

SUB-CATEGORY
Books, Newspapers and Magazines

DIVISION
Temporary

AWARD
Silver

TITLE
Disney Publishing Spinner

CLIENT
Disney Children's Publishing
Division

ENTRANT
The Display Connection, Inc.
Moonachie, NJ

SUB-CATEGORY
Books, Newspapers and
Magazines

DIVISION
Permanent

AWARD
Silver

TITLE
Duracell Modular
Countertop Display

CLIENT
The Gillette Company

ENTRANT
Display Producers, Inc.
Bronx, NY

SUB-CATEGORY
Film and Batteries
(including disposable or fun
cameras)

DIVISION
Permanent

AWARD
Silver

TITLE
Lego Media 2-Sided Floor
Stand

CLIENT
Lego Media International, Inc.

ENTRANT
Design Phase, Inc.
Northbrook, IL

SUB-CATEGORY
Games

DIVISION
Permanent

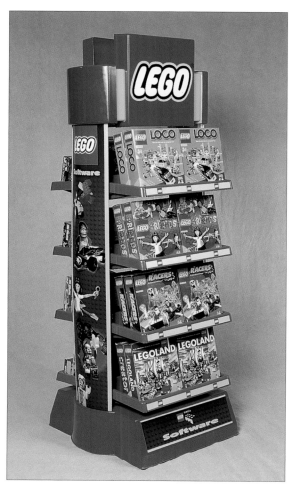

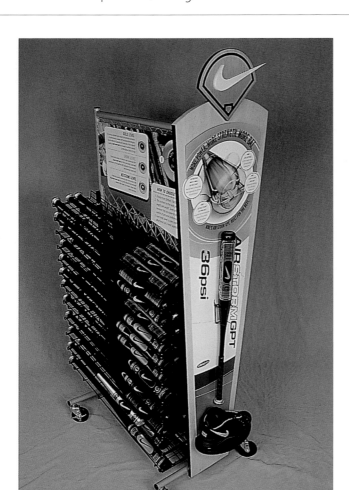

AWARD
Silver

TITLE
Nike Baseball/Softball Fixture

CLIENT
Nike Inc

ENTRANT
Cormark
Elk Grove Village, IL

SUB-CATEGORY
Sports Equipment
(including bicycles, etc.)

DIVISION
Permanent

AWARD
Silver

TITLE
Spalding Basketball Floor Display

CLIENT
Spalding Sports Worldwide, Inc.

ENTRANT
Einson Freeman
Paramus, NJ

SUB-CATEGORY
Sports Equipment
(including bicycles, etc.)

DIVISION
Permanent

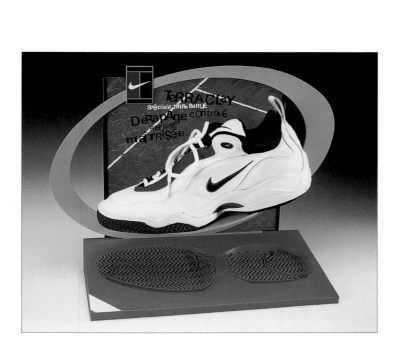

AWARD
Silver

TITLE
Nike Terra Clay Counter Display

CLIENT
Nike

ENTRANT
Diam Groupe
Les Mureaux, Cedex, France

SUB-CATEGORY
Sports Equipment
(including bicycles, etc.)

DIVISION
Semi-Permanent

AWARD
Silver

TITLE
Droideka

CLIENT
DK Publishing

ENTRANT
Advanced Graphics One
Studio City, CA

SUB-CATEGORY
Books, Newspapers
and Magazines

DIVISION
Temporary

AWARD
Silver

TITLE
Space Encyclopedia
Lectern

CLIENT
Dorling Kindersley

ENTRANT
Rand Display, Inc.
Teaneck, NJ

SUB-CATEGORY
Books, Newspapers
and Magazines

DIVISION
Temporary

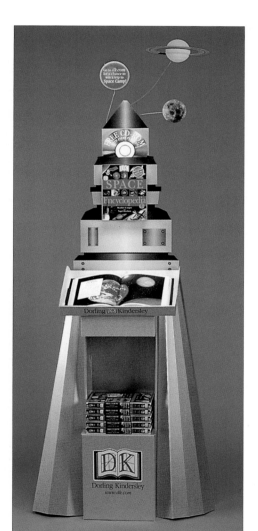

AWARD
Silver

TITLE
The Complete Home
Medical Guide

CLIENT
Dorling Kindersley

ENTRANT
Rand Display, Inc.
Teaneck, NJ

SUB-CATEGORY
Books, Newspapers
and Magazines

DIVISION
Temporary

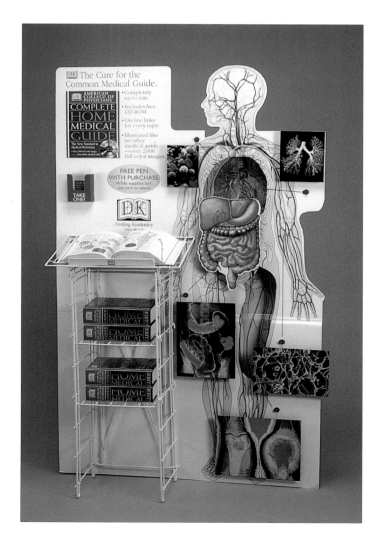

AWARD
Silver

TITLE
Alkaline 1/4 Pallet Display

CLIENT
Panasonic Industrial Co.

ENTRANT
Advertising Display Company
Lyndhurst, NJ

SUB-CATEGORY
Film and Batteries
(including disposable or fun cameras)

DIVISION
Temporary

AWARD
Silver

TITLE
Toy Story II Action
Toy Zone Merchandiser

CLIENT
Mattel Toys

ENTRANT
Taurus Packaging
Cherry Hill, NJ

SUB-CATEGORY
Toys

DIVISION
Temporary

AWARD
Silver

TITLE
Titleist 24 Dozen HP Intro Display

CLIENT
Titleist/Foot Joy Worldwide

ENTRANT
Triangle Display Group
Philadelphia, PA

SUB-CATEGORY
Sports Equipment
(including bicycles, etc.)

DIVISION
Temporary

AWARD
Bronze

TITLE
Wilson Fat Shaft Torque Display

CLIENT
Wilson Sporting Goods

ENTRANT
Cormark
Elk Grove Village, IL

SUB-CATEGORY
Sports Equipment
(including bicycles, etc.)

DIVISION
Permanent

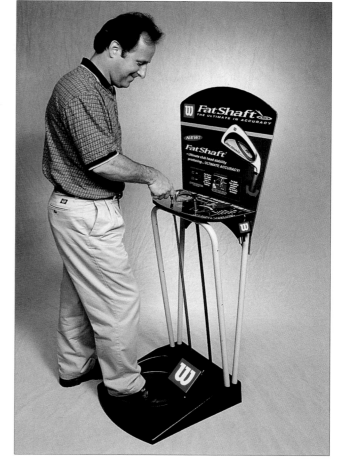

AWARD
Bronze

TITLE
Hyper Carbon Backwall

CLIENT
Wilson Sporting Goods

ENTRANT
Great Northern Corporation
Racine, WI

SUB-CATEGORY
Sports Equipment
(including bicycles, etc.)

DIVISION
Permanent

AWARD
Bronze

TITLE
K2 Snowboards
Slat Wall System

CLIENT
K2 Snowboards

ENTRANT
JP Marketiing Services
Sante Fe Springs, CA

SUB-CATEGORY
Sports Equipment
(including bicycles, etc.)

DIVISION
Permanent

AWARD
Bronze

TITLE
Body Geometry Saddle Display

CLIENT
Specialized Bicycle Components

ENTRANT
Rapid Displays
Union City, CA

SUB-CATEGORY
Sports Equipment
(including bicycles, etc.)

DIVISION
Permanent

AWARD
Bronze

TITLE
Lincoln Logs Shelf Topper

CLIENT
K'Nex Industries

ENTRANT
Taurus Packaging
Cherry Hill, NJ

SUB-CATEGORY
Toys

DIVISION
Permanent

AWARD
Bronze

TITLE
Lego Three Mini Figures

CLIENT
Lego Systems, Inc.

ENTRANT
Design Phase, Inc.
Northbrook, IL

SUB-CATEGORY
Toys

DIVISION
Permanent

AWARD
Bronze

TITLE
St. Martin's Press Encarta

CLIENT
St. Martin's Press

ENTRANT
Taurus Packaging
Cherry Hill, NJ

SUB-CATEGORY
Books, Newspapers and Magazines

DIVISION
Semi-Permanent

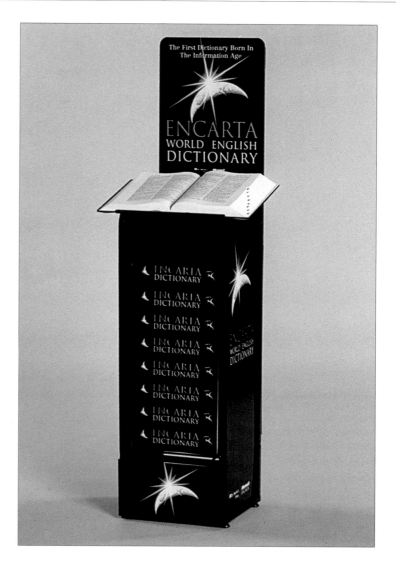

AWARD
Bronze

TITLE
Titleist 8 Dozen HP Intro
Display

CLIENT
Titleist/Foot Joy World
Wide

ENTRANT
Triangle Display Group
Philadelphia, PA

SUB-CATEGORY
Sports Equipment
(including bicycles, etc.)

DIVISION
Semi-Permanent

AWARD
Bronze

TITLE
R2D2

CLIENT
DK Publishing

ENTRANT
Advanced Graphics One
STUDIO CITY, CA

SUB-CATEGORY
Books, Newspapers and
Magazines

DIVISION
Temporary

AWARD
Bronze

TITLE
Battle Droid

CLIENT
DK Publishing

ENTRANT
Advanced Graphics One
Studio City, CA

SUB-CATEGORY
Books, Newspapers
and Magazines

DIVISION
Temporary

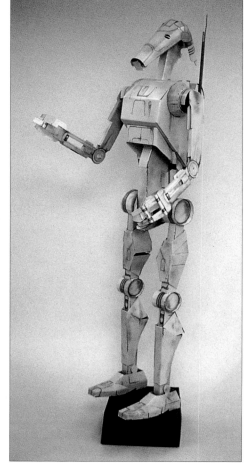

AWARD
Bronze

TITLE
Pit Droid

CLIENT
DK Publishing

ENTRANT
Advanced Graphics One
Studio City, CA

SUB-CATEGORY
Books, Newspapers
and Magazines"

DIVISION
Temporary

AWARD
Bronze

TITLE
Pod Racers

CLIENT
DK Publishing

ENTRANT
Advanced Graphics One
Studio City, CA

SUB-CATEGORY
Books, Newspapers
and Magazines

DIVISION
Temporary

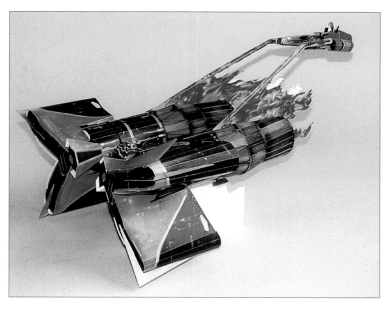

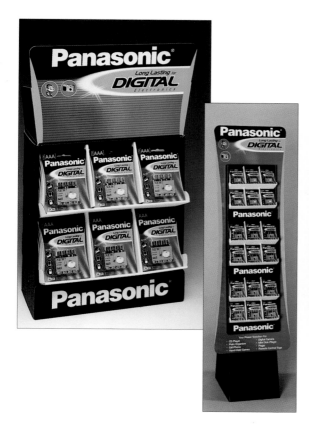

AWARD
Bronze

TITLE
Digital Battery FS/PW/CD

CLIENT
Panasonic Industrial Co.

ENTRANT
Advertising Display Company
Lyndhurst, NJ

SUB-CATEGORY
Film and Batteries
(including disposable or fun cameras)

DIVISION
Temporary

AWARD
Bronze

TITLE
The 2000 Old Farmer's
Almanac 60/24 Large

CLIENT
Yankee Publishing, Inc.

ENTRANT
Triangle Display Group
Philadelphia, PA

SUB-CATEGORY
Books, Newspapers
and Magazines

DIVISION
Temporary

AWARD
Bronze

TITLE
Duracell/Wal-Mart Rolling Display

CLIENT
Duracell USA

ENTRANT
Chesapeake Display & Packaging
Winston Salem, NC

SUB-CATEGORY
Film and Batteries
(including disposable or fun cameras)

DIVISION
Temporary

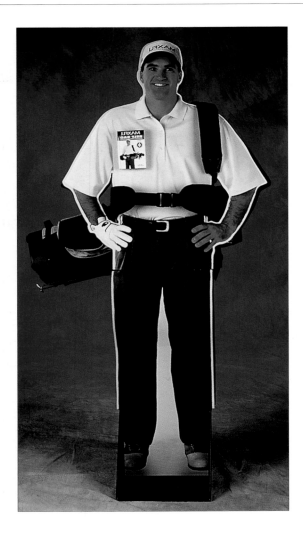

AWARD
Bronze

TITLE
Maxfli Belt Golf Bag Standee

CLIENT
Maxfli

ENTRANT
Inland Consumer Packaging and Displays
Indianapolis, IN

SUB-CATEGORY
Sports Equipment (including bicycles, etc.)

DIVISION
Temporary

AWARD
Bronze

TITLE
Titleist 20 Dozen
Tower Display

CLIENT
Titleist/Foot Joy World
Wide

ENTRANT
Triangle Display Group
Philadelphia, PA

SUB-CATEGORY
Sports Equipment
(including bicycles, etc.)

DIVISION
Temporary

AWARD
Bronze

TITLE
Mattel Kid's Puzzles 1/2 Pallet

CLIENT
Mattel Toys

ENTRANT
Taurus Packaging
Cherry Hill, NJ

SUB-CATEGORY
Toys

DIVISION
Temporary

AWARD
Bronze

TITLE
Star Wars Floor Display

CLIENT
Lego Systems, Inc.

ENTRANT
Triangle Display Group
Philadelphia, PA

SUB-CATEGORY
Toys

DIVISION
Temporary

AWARD
Bronze

TITLE
Throwbots Floor Display

CLIENT
Lego Systems, Inc.

ENTRANT
Triangle Display Group
Philadelphia, PA

SUB-CATEGORY
Toys

DIVISION
Temporary

AWARD
Bronze

TITLE
Mania 2000 Floor Display

CLIENT
Lego Systems, Inc.

ENTRANT
Triangle Display Group
Philadelphia, PA

SUB-CATEGORY
Toys

DIVISION
Temporary

AWARD
Gold

TITLE
Office Depot Stamp and Sign Display

CLIENT
Identity Group, Inc.

ENTRANT
R/P Creative Sales, Inc.
Burbank, CA

SUB-CATEGORY
Office Equipment and Supplies

DIVISION
Permanent

AWARD
Gold

TITLE
Bic Schoolhouse Pallet
Display

CLIENT
Bic Corporation

ENTRANT
Triangle Display Group
Philadelphia, PA

SUB-CATEGORY
Stationery, Party Goods,
Giftwrap, Disposable
Writing Instruments
and Seasonal Items

DIVISION
Semi-Permanent

AWARD
Gold

TITLE
Halloween Large Theme Display

CLIENT
M&M/Mars

ENTRANT
Smurfit-Stone Display Group
Richmond, VA

SUB-CATEGORY
Stationery, Party Goods, Giftwrap,
Disposable Writing Instruments and
Seasonal Items

DIVISION
Temporary

AWARD
Silver

TITLE
3M Permanent Clip Strip
for Post-it & Scotch

CLIENT
3M Stationery and Office Supplies

ENTRANT
Trans World Marketing
East Rutherford, NJ

SUB-CATEGORY
Office Equipment and Supplies

DIVISION
Permanent

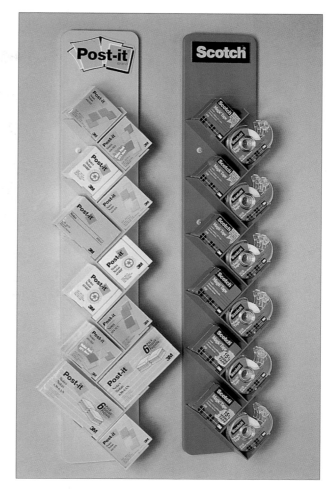

AWARD
Silver

TITLE
Office Depot 2000 Island Display

CLIENT
At-A-Glance

ENTRANT
Rand Display, Inc.
Teaneck, NJ

SUB-CATEGORY
Stationery, Party Goods, Giftwrap, Disposable
Writing Instruments and Seasonal Items

DIVISION
Permanent

AWARD
Silver

TITLE
Things Remembered Ornament Display

CLIENT
Things Remembered

ENTRANT
RCS, an American Greetings Company
Cleveland, OH

SUB-CATEGORY
Stationery, Party Goods, Giftwrap, Disposable
Writing Instruments and Seasonal Items

DIVISION
Semi-Permanent

AWARD
Silver

TITLE
Christman Large Theme
Display

CLIENT
M&M/Mars

ENTRANT
Smurfit-Stone Display Group
Richmond, VA

SUB-CATEGORY
Stationery, Party Goods,
Giftwrap, Disposable Writing
Instruments and Seasonal Items

DIVISION
Temporary

AWARD
Silver

TITLE
Walmart Full Pallet

CLIENT
Manco, Inc.

ENTRANT
Packaging Corporation of
America
Ashland, OH

SUB-CATEGORY
Office Equipment and Supplies

DIVISION
Temporary

AWARD
Bronze

TITLE
Intuitions Outpost

CLIENT
American Greetings

ENTRANT
American Greetings
Cleveland, OH

SUB-CATEGORY
Greeting Cards
(including seasonal)

DIVISION
Permanent

AWARD
Bronze

TITLE
Gillette/Staples Writing Center

CLIENT
The Gillette Company

ENTRANT
Henschel-Steinau, Inc.
Englewood, NJ

SUB-CATEGORY
Office Equipment and Supplies

DIVISION
Permanent

AWARD
Bronze

TITLE
Learning Company/Staples Spinner

CLIENT
Learning Company

ENTRANT
CDA Industries Inc.
Scarborough, ON, Canada

SUB-CATEGORY
Office Equipment and Supplies

DIVISION
Permanent

AWARD
Bronze

TITLE
Party Essentials Spinner

CLIENT
American Greetings

ENTRANT
American Greetings
Cleveland, OH

SUB-CATEGORY
Stationery, Party Goods, Giftwrap, Disposable
Writing Instruments and Seasonal Items

DIVISION
Permanent

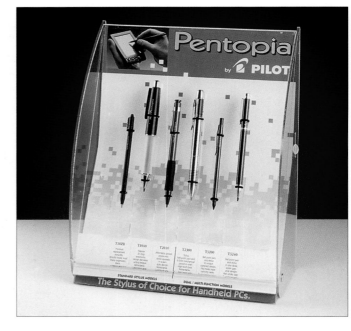

AWARD
Bronze

TITLE
Avery Tax Time Binder Pallet
Display

CLIENT
Avery Dennison

ENTRANT
Longview Fibre DisplayGroup
Milwaukee, WI

SUB-CATEGORY
Office Equipment and Supplies

DIVISION
Temporary

AWARD
Bronze

TITLE
Pentopia Counter Display

CLIENT
Pilot Pen Corporation of
America

ENTRANT
P.O.P. Displays International
Woodside, NY

SUB-CATEGORY
Stationery, Party Goods,
Giftwrap, Disposable Writing
Instruments and Seasonal Items

DIVISION
Permanent

AWARD
Bronze

TITLE
Sesame Street Endcap Display

CLIENT
American Greetings

ENTRANT
American Greetings
Cleveland, OH

SUB-CATEGORY
Stationery, Party Goods, Giftwrap, Disposable
Writing Instruments and Seasonal Items

DIVISION
Temporary

AWARD
Bronze

TITLE
Bic EZ Stroke Powerwing

CLIENT
Bic Corporation

ENTRANT
Triangle Display Group
Philadelphia, PA

SUB-CATEGORY
Office Equipment and Supplies

DIVISION
Temporary

AWARD
Bronze

TITLE
Frankie Halloween Standee

CLIENT
KMart Corporation

ENTRANT
RCS, an American Greetings Company
Cleveland, OH

SUB-CATEGORY
Stationery, Party Goods, Giftwrap, Disposable
Writing Instruments and Seasonal Items

DIVISION
Temporary

AWARD
Gold

TITLE
Camel Pleasure to Burn Campaign

CLIENT
R.J. Reynolds Tobacco Company

ENTRANT
Corrflex Display & Packaging
Statesville, CT

SUB-CATEGORY
Cigarettes - Non-Illuminated

DIVISION
Temporary

AWARD
Gold

TITLE
Parliament multi-level illuminated sign

CLIENT
The Phillip Morris Company

ENTRANT
Thomson-Leeds Company Inc.
Sunnyside, NY

SUB-CATEGORY
Cigarettes - Illuminated

DIVISION
Permanent

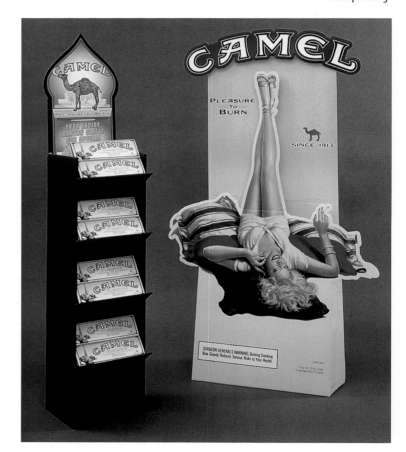

AWARD
Gold

TITLE
Doral "Take A Taste Drive" Counter
Display

CLIENT
R.J. Reynolds Tobacco Company

ENTRANT
Rock-Tenn Company/ Alliance Group
Winston Salem, NC

SUB-CATEGORY
Cigarettes - Non-Illuminated

DIVISION
Temporary

AWARD
Gold

TITLE
Camel Ultra Lights 20 Pack Display

CLIENT
R.J. Reynolds Tobacco Company

ENTRANT
Rock-Tenn Company/ Alliance Group
Winston Salem, NC

SUB-CATEGORY
Cigarettes - Non-Illuminated

DIVISION
Temporary

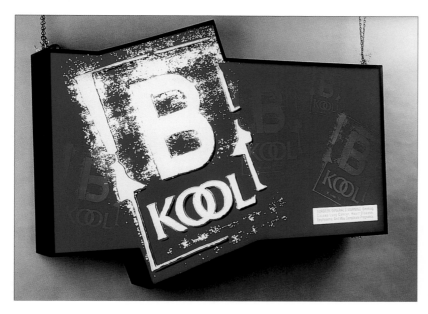

AWARD
Silver

TITLE
Kool Lightmaster Supersign

CLIENT
Brown & Williamson Tobacco

ENTRANT
CDA Industries Inc.
Scarborough, ON, Canada

SUB-CATEGORY
Cigarettes - Illuminated

DIVISION
Permanent

AWARD
Silver

TITLE
Multi-Brand Cigarette
Merchandiser

CLIENT
Imperial Tobacco Limited

ENTRANT
Admark Display Ltd.
Scarborough, ON, Canada

SUB-CATEGORY
Cigarettes - Non-Illuminated

DIVISION
Permanent

AWARD
Silver

TITLE
Doral 2" x 2" Multi-Image Motion Sign

CLIENT
R.J. Reynolds Tobacco Company

ENTRANT
Rapid Displays
Chicago, IL

SUB-CATEGORY
Cigarettes - Non-Illuminated

DIVISION
Permanent

AWARD
Silver

TITLE
Camel Wind Spinner

CLIENT
R.J. Reynolds Tobacco Company

ENTRANT
ImageWorks Display & Marketing Group
Winston Salem, NC

SUB-CATEGORY
Cigarettes - Non-Illuminated

DIVISION
Semi-Permanent

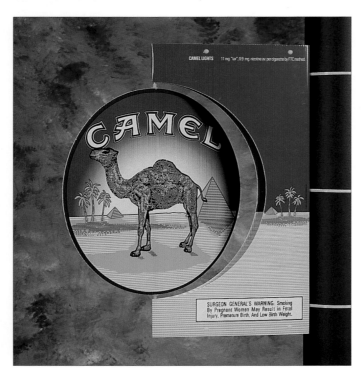

AWARD
Silver

TITLE
Bering Carousel Display

CLIENT
Swisher International, Inc.

ENTRANT
E-B Display Company, Inc.
Massilon, OH

SUB-CATEGORY
Other Tobacco Products
(smokeless tobacco, cigars, etc.)

DIVISION
Permanent

AWARD
Silver

TITLE
Twenty Can Facsimile Vendor

CLIENT
United States Tobacco

ENTRANT
resources in display
Cranford, NJ

SUB-CATEGORY
Other Tobacco Products
(smokeless tobacco, cigars, etc.)

DIVISION
Semi-Permanent

AWARD
Bronze

TITLE
Parliament gravity feed display

CLIENT
The Phillip Morris Company

ENTRANT
Thomson-Leeds Company Inc.
Sunnyside, NY

SUB-CATEGORY
Cigarettes - Non-Illuminated

DIVISION
Permanent

AWARD
Bronze

TITLE
Camel Pool Table Light

CLIENT
R.J. Reynolds Tobacco Co.

ENTRANT
KCS Industries, Inc.
Hartland, WI

SUB-CATEGORY
Cigarettes - Illuminated

DIVISION
Permanent

AWARD
Bronze

TITLE
Parliament Sequencing
neon

CLIENT
Philip Morris U.S.A.

ENTRANT
Everbrite, Inc.
Greenfield, WI

SUB-CATEGORY
Cigarettes - Illuminated

DIVISION
Permanent

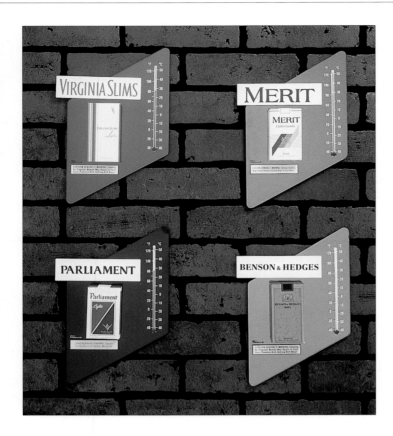

AWARD
Bronze

TITLE
Phillip Morris indoor-outdoor thermometers

CLIENT
The Phillip Morris Company

ENTRANT
Thomson-Leeds Company Inc.
Sunnyside, NY

SUB-CATEGORY
Cigarettes - Non-Illuminated

DIVISION
Permanent

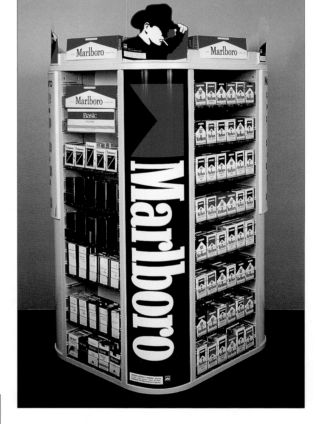

AWARD
Bronze

TITLE
Phillip Morris Center Island Spinner

CLIENT
The Phillip Morris Company

ENTRANT
Thomson-Leeds Company Inc.
Sunnyside, NY

SUB-CATEGORY
Cigarettes - Non-Illuminated

DIVISION
Permanent

AWARD
Bronze

TITLE
RJR Ceiling Pricer Sign Program

CLIENT
R.J. Reynolds Tobacco
Company

ENTRANT
Trans World Marketing
East Rutherford, NJ

SUB-CATEGORY
Cigarettes - Non-Illuminated

DIVISION
Permanent

AWARD
Bronze

TITLE
Timber Wolf Mirror

CLIENT
Swedish Match of North
America

ENTRANT
Heritage Sign & Display
Nesquehoning, PA

SUB-CATEGORY
Other Tobacco Products
(smokeless tobacco, cigars, etc.)

DIVISION
Permanent

AWARD
Bronze

TITLE
Tobacco Galleria Counter Display

CLIENT
Consolidated Cigar Corporation

ENTRANT
ImageWorks Display & Marketing
Group
Winston Salem, NC

SUB-CATEGORY
Other Tobacco Products
(smokeless tobacco, cigars, etc.)

DIVISION
Permanent

AWARD
Bronze

TITLE
Memphis Blue Launch
Instore

CLIENT
Austria Tabak Scandinavia

ENTRANT
Ajax Active
Stockholm, Sweden

SUB-CATEGORY
Cigarettes - Non-Illuminated

DIVISION
Semi-Permanent

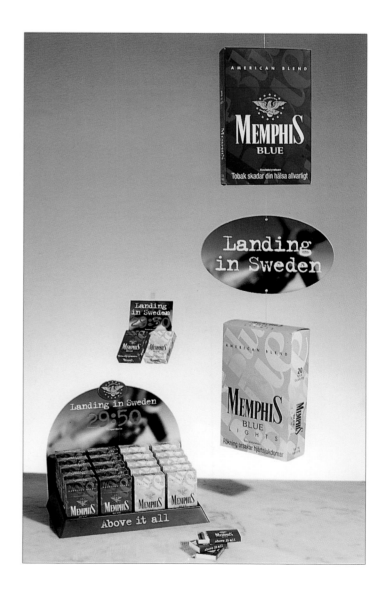

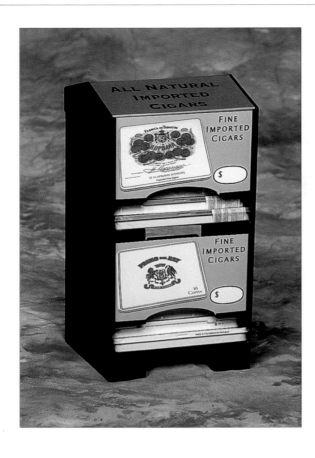

AWARD
Bronze

TITLE
Cigar Tin Gravity Feed Display

CLIENT
Consolidated Cigar Corporation

ENTRANT
ImageWorks Display &
Marketing Group
Winston Salem, NC

SUB-CATEGORY
Other Tobacco Products
(smokeless tobacco, cigars, etc.)

DIVISION
Semi-Permanent

AWARD
Bronze

TITLE
Red Kamel Collector's
Tin C-top/Easel Card

CLIENT
R.J. Reynolds Tobacco
Company

ENTRANT
Corrflex Display & Packaging
Statesville, NC

SUB-CATEGORY
Cigarettes - Non-Illuminated

DIVISION
Temporary

AWARD
Bronze

TITLE
Red Seal 25% More
Counter Display

CLIENT
United States Tobacco

ENTRANT
resources in display
Cranford, NJ

SUB-CATEGORY
Other Tobacco Products
(smokeless tobacco, cigars, etc.)

DIVISION
Semi-Permanent

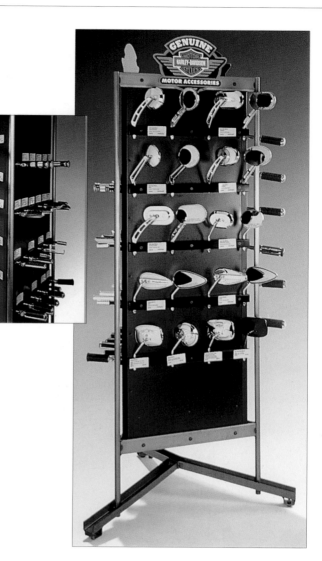

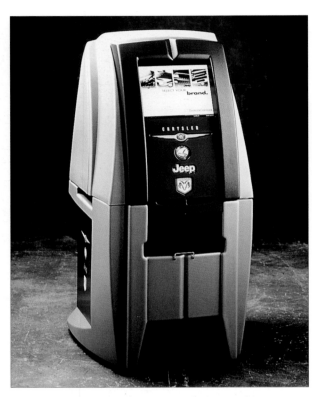

AWARD
Silver

TITLE
Brand Kiosk

CLIENT
Daimler Chrysler

ENTRANT
Visual Productions
Troy, MI

SUB-CATEGORY
Passenger Cars and
Specialty Vehicles

DIVISION
Permanent

AWARD
Bronze

TITLE
Honda Security Systems Interactive Display

CLIENT
American Honda Motor Co. Inc.

ENTRANT
R/P Creative Sales, Inc.
Burbank, CA

SUB-CATEGORY
Automotive Aftermarket
(including tires, batteries, accessories, waxes and
washes, polishers and socket wrenches, etc.)

DIVISION
Permanent

AWARD
Bronze

TITLE
Warn Step Display

CLIENT
Warn Industries

ENTRANT
Rapid Displays
Union City, IL

SUB-CATEGORY
Automotive Aftermarket
(including tires, batteries, accessories,
waxes and washes, polishers and
socket wrenches, etc.)

DIVISION
Permanent

AWARD
Bronze

TITLE
Goodyear "Fluids Changeover" Display

CLIENT
Goodyear Tire & Rubber Company

ENTRANT
Tusco Display
Gnadenhutten, OH

SUB-CATEGORY
Automotive Aftermarket
(including tires, batteries, accessories,
waxes and washes, polishers and
socket wrenches, etc.)

DIVISION
Permanent

AWARD
Bronze

TITLE
Mercury Marine MercuryCare Program

CLIENT
Mercury Marine

ENTRANT
DCI Marketing
Milwaukee, WI

SUB-CATEGORY
Passenger Cars and Specialty Vehicles

DIVISION
Permanent

AWARD
Bronze

TITLE
Suzuki Information Center

CLIENT
American Suzuki Motor Corp.

ENTRANT
R/P Creative Sales, Inc.
Burbank, CA

SUB-CATEGORY
Passenger Cars and Specialty Vehicles

DIVISION
Permanent

AWARD
Bronze

TITLE
Statoil Engine Oil Display

CLIENT
Statoil Denmark

ENTRANT
Leo Burnett Oslo
Oslo, Norway

SUB-CATEGORY
Petroleum Products

DIVISION
Temporary

Multinational
Awards Contest

The Multinational Contest recognizes
the merchandising excellence of
displays produced and placed outside
the United States, Europe and Japan.

AWARD
Gold

TITLE
Oral Health Care Center

CLIENT
Colgate Palmolive

ENTRANT
Frank Mayer & Associates, Inc.
Grafton, WI

SUB-CATEGORY
Multinational

DIVISION
Permanent

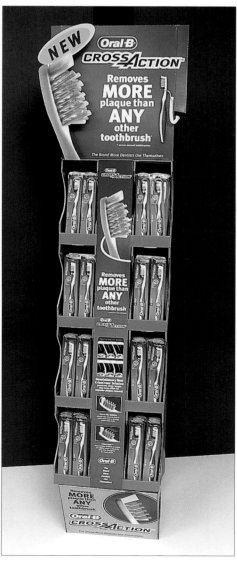

AWARD
Gold

TITLE
Gillette Oral B
Cross Action Display

CLIENT
Gillette Australia

ENTRANT
Visy Displays
Reservoir, Victoria, Australia

SUB-CATEGORY
Multinational

DIVISION
Semi-Permanent

AWARD
Gold/Display-of-the-Year

TITLE
Kit Kat Bonus Break
Merchandiser

CLIENT
Nestle Confectionery Ltd

ENTRANT
Ace Print & Display Pty Ltd
Revesby, Australia

SUB-CATEGORY
Multinational

DIVISION
Temporary

AWARD
Silver

TITLE
Play Station Self-Standing Display

CLIENT
Sat Kartar Enterprises

ENTRANT
Armo Diseno S.A. De C.V,
Mexico City, D.F., Mexico

SUB-CATEGORY
Multinational

DIVISION
Permanent

AWARD
Silver

TITLE
Cadbury Crème Egg Display

CLIENT
Cadbury Schweppes
Confectionery Division

ENTRANT
Amcor Fibre Packaging
Box Hill, Victoria, Australia

SUB-CATEGORY
Multinational

DIVISION
Semi-Permanent

AWARD
Silver

TITLE
Disney Video Merchandising
System

CLIENT
Buena Vista Home
Entertainment (Mexico)

ENTRANT
MZM
San Bartolo, Naucalpan, Mexico

SUB-CATEGORY
Multinational

DIVISION
Permanent

AWARD
Silver

TITLE
Holiday Extras 20's Giant Cigarette Pack

CLIENT
Rothmans of Pall Mall (Australia)
Limited

ENTRANT
Display Packaging Pty Ltd
Mosman, Australia

SUB-CATEGORY
Multinational

DIVISION
Semi-Permanent

AWARD
Silver

TITLE
Axe hypnotic Self-Standing
Display

CLIENT
Unilever de México S.A. de C.V.

ENTRANT
Armo Diseno S.A. De C.V,
Mexico City, D.F., Mexico

SUB-CATEGORY
Multinational

DIVISION
Temporary

AWARD
Silver

TITLE
Rexona Hanging Display

CLIENT
Unilever de México S.A. de C.V.

ENTRANT
Armo Diseno S.A. De C.V,.
Mexico City, D.F., Mexico

SUB-CATEGORY
Multinational

DIVISION
Temporary

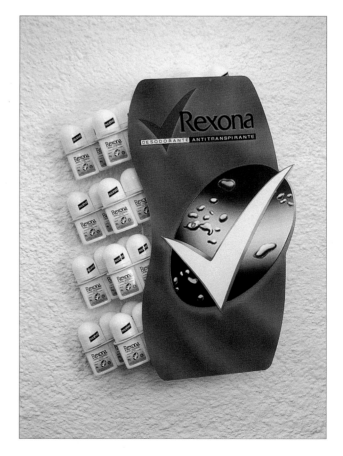

AWARD
Bronze

TITLE
Mobile Phone Instore Display

CLIENT
Vodafone Pty Ltd

ENTRANT
Efficiency Displays (Marketing) Pty Ltd
Brookvale, Australia

SUB-CATEGORY
Multinational

DIVISION
Permanent

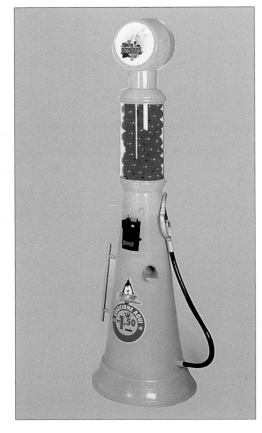

AWARD
Bronze

TITLE
Shell Cartoon Mania

CLIENT
Shell Brasil S/A

ENTRANT
Oficina de Merchandising Ind.Com. Ltda
Sao Paulo, Brazil

SUB-CATEGORY
Multinational

DIVISION
Permanent

AWARD
Bronze

TITLE
Equipment Predator Accelerator
Shoe Display

CLIENT
adidas International

ENTRANT
Rapid Displays
Union City, CA

SUB-CATEGORY
Multinational

DIVISION
Permanent

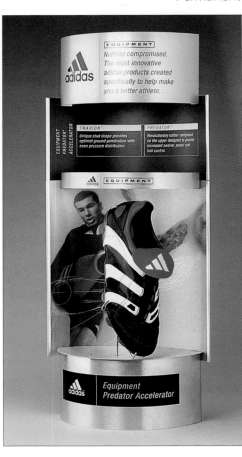

AWARD
Bronze

TITLE
Tine "Operation Shelf Storm"

CLIENT
Tine Norwegian Dairies BA

ENTRANT
Leo Burnett Oslo
Oslo, Norway

SUB-CATEGORY
Multinational

DIVISION
Semi-Permanent

AWARD
Bronze

TITLE
Gillette Costco Canada
Pallet Display

CLIENT
The Gillette Company

ENTRANT
New Dimensions Research
Corporation
Melville, NY

SUB-CATEGORY
Multinational

DIVISION
Semi-Permanent

AWARD
Bronze

TITLE
Mars Starburst Juice Station

CLIENT
Mars Confectionary

ENTRANT
Visy Displays
Reservoir, Victoria, Australia

SUB-CATEGORY
Multinational

DIVISION
Semi-Permanent

AWARD
Bronze

TITLE
Invite Dare To The Party

CLIENT
Dare Foods

ENTRANT
Lyton Promotion
Development Group
Toronto, ON, Canada

SUB-CATEGORY
Multinational

DIVISION

AWARD
Bronze

TITLE
Nabisco Cool Bus Displayer

CLIENT
Nabisco

ENTRANT
Protagon Display Inc.
Scarborough, ON, Canada

SUB-CATEGORY
Multinational

DIVISION
Temporary

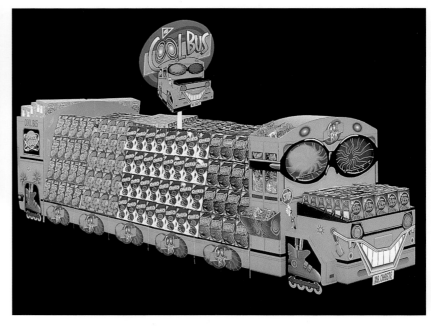

AWARD
Bronze

TITLE
Let's Party 1999/2000

CLIENT
Snack Brands Australia

ENTRANT
Visy Displays
Smithfield, NSW, Australia

SUB-CATEGORY
Multinational

DIVISION
Temporary

Technical
Awards Contest

POPAI's Technical Awards recognize engineering excellence and the innovative use of materials in P-O-P design.

AWARD
Gold

TITLE
FrigoPub Nestle Buitoni Italian Meal Centre

CLIENT
Nestle U.S.A.

ENTRANT
Octagon Industries Inc.
Toronto, ON, Canada

SUB-CATEGORY
Supermarkets

DIVISION
Temporary

AWARD
Gold

TITLE
Coca-Cola license Premise Illuminated Sign

CLIENT
Coca-Cola South Pacific Pty Ltd

ENTRANT
Airform Int'l & Wellington Screen Print Ltd
Christchurch, Canterbury, New Zealand

SUB-CATEGORY
Soft Drinks, Mineral Waters and
Powdered Mixes

DIVISION
Permanent

AWARD
Silver

TITLE
Thermasilk Lenticular Floorstand

CLIENT
Unilever Home & Personal Care USA

ENTRANT
Phoenix Display/International Paper
Thorofare, NJ

SUB-CATEGORY
Hair Cleansing Treatments
(including shampoos and
conditioners, etc.)

DIVISION
Temporary

AWARD
Silver

TITLE
Bud 4th of July Motion

CLIENT
Anheuser-Busch, Inc.

ENTRANT
Rapid Displays
Chicago, IL

SUB-CATEGORY
Off-Premise - Illuminated
or Motion

DIVISION
Temporary

AWARD
Silver

TITLE
Home Depot Pivot Signage System

CLIENT
The Home Depot

ENTRANT
Cormark
Elk Grove Village, IL

SUB-CATEGORY
Signage Category

DIVISION
Permanent

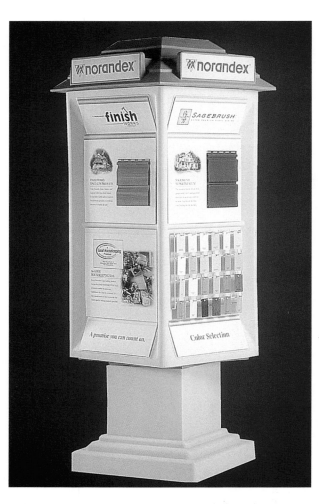

Award
Silver

Title
Norandex Rotating Vinyl Siding Display

Client
Norandex/Reynolds Distribution Company

Entrant
PFI Displays, Inc.
Rittman, OH

Sub-Category
Building Supplies
(including paints and stains, paneling, ceiling
tiles, lighting and fixtures, roofing materials,
lumber, siding, heating, plumbing, etc.)

Division
Permanent

Award
Bronze

Title
Clean and Clear Floor Dislay

Client
Johnson & Johnson

Entrant
Techno P.O.S. inc.
Anjou, PQ, Canada

Sub-Category
Skin Care Products
(including cleansers, shaving
creams, aftershaves, etc.)

Division
Temporary

Award
Bronze

Title
R2D2

Client
DK Publishing

Entrant
Advanced Graphics One
Studio City, CA

Sub-Category
Books, Newspapers and
Magazines

Division
Temporary

TITLE
Dewar's Holiday Mass Merchandiser

CLIENT
Bacardi Martini Promotions

ENTRANT
Protagon Display Inc.
Scarborough, ON, Canada

SUB-CATEGORY
Distilled Spirits - Illuminated or Motion

DIVISION
Temporary

AWARD
Bronze

TITLE
IntelliMouse Explorer Marquee

CLIENT
Microsoft

ENTRANT
Promo Edge Division of Menasha Corporation
Menomonee Falls, WI

SUB-CATEGORY
Signage Category

DIVISION
Semi-Permanent

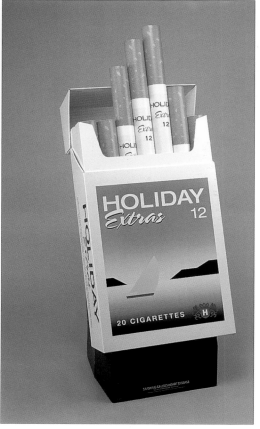

AWARD
Bronze

TITLE
Holiday Extras 20's Giant
Cigarette Pack

CLIENT
Rothmans of Pall Mall
(Australia) Limited

ENTRANT
Display Packaging Pty Ltd
Mosman, Australia

SUB-CATEGORY
Multinational

DIVISION
Semi-Permanent

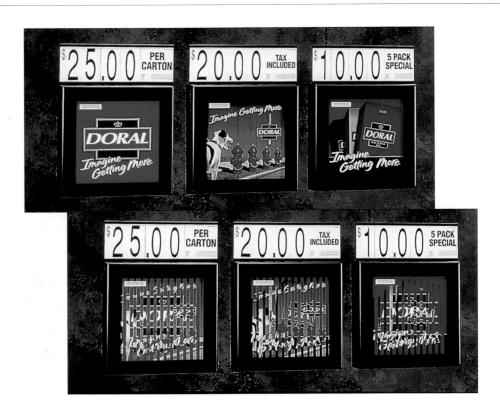

AWARD
Bronze

TITLE
Doral 2" x 2" Multi-Image Motion Sign

CLIENT
R.J. Reynolds Tobacco Co.

ENTRANT
Rapid Displays
Chicago, IL

SUB-CATEGORY
Cigarettes - Non-Illuminated

DIVISION
Permanent

AWARD
Bronze

TITLE
Lucky Strike Outdoor Ash Can

CLIENT
Brown & Williamson Tobacco

ENTRANT
Brown & Williamson Tobacco
Louisville, KY

SUB-CATEGORY
Cigarettes - Non-Illuminated

DIVISION
Permanent

AWARD
Bronze

TITLE
Duracell Spinners

CLIENT
Duracell

ENTRANT
New Dimensions Research
Corporation
Melville, NY

SUB-CATEGORY
Film and Batteries
(including disposable or fun cameras)

DIVISION
Permanent

Index of Displays